On the Wings of Spirit

The Further Musings of a Soul
On Her Journey Homeward

by Rebecca Zinn

Uni✶Sun
Kansas City

This book is manufactured in the United States of America. Distribution
by The Talman Company:

The Talman Co.
150 Fifth Avenue
New York, NY 10011

ISBN 0-912949-21-X
Library of Congress Catalog Card Number 88-051048

A
Uni★Sun
BOOK
Distributed by
THE TALMAN COMPANY

to Victor & Josh

Contents

INTRODUCTION

My father died on the last day of June in 1983. Twelve hours later on the first day of July, my spiritual journey began. Unlike many contemporary seekers, I had not attended seminars or workshops looking for truth and enlightenment; I had never sought guidance from the Tarot, the *I Ching*, or Celtic runes; and I did not yet have a bookshelf filled with books like this one. Before Dad died I was an ordinary skeptic, an Average American Agnostic. I thought astrology was somewhat silly and crystals were merely shiny rocks. Meditation was entirely too sedate an endeavor to excite my interest. I had never heard of channeling, but I thought communication with disembodied souls was a rather foolish parlor game practiced only by women much older than I who could find no better way to entertain themselves than to sit around a crystal ball invoking dead people. In my opinion it was mostly, if not totally, naive folly. During that phase of my life, I counsidered myself entirely too educated, sophisticated, and intellectually mature for escapades into the esoteric or flights of fantasy into Lala Land.

Suddenly and without warning, my father developed cancer. For a while, I hoped for miracles, but people whose cancer has spread rampantly throughout their bodies and their brains are not the most likely candidates for miraculous cure. Gradually I released my hopes for medical miracles, and as I did, I began to notice a sparkle in my father's eyes that I'd never seen there before. I began to feel calmer than usual in his presence. I began to understand that not all miracles bring gifts of physical healing; some bring gifts to the heart even as the body fades. Dad's entire demeanor changed as he approached his death, becoming quietly radiant and almost angelic. Surprisingly, I had no fear of his death. Even more surprisingly, neither did he. Instead of seeing fear in his dying eyes, I saw deeper tenderness and peace than I had ever seen in the eyes of another person.

The big surprises and little miracles that my family experienced as Dad died were precious, but they were not potent enough to overpower the deeply ingrained doubt and skepticism that pervaded my religious and spiritual beliefs. As a clincial psychologist, I had often observed that when people find themselves in stressful situations, unusual things happen—unusual things that sometimes seem nearly miraculous. Even though little miracles occurred rather often, I expected that after Dad's death, life would return to the state I then considered to be normal. If it had not been for what happened the morning after my father's death, I imagine that life would have returned to normal and that I would have tenderly tucked away all the little miracles of the previous months, interpreting them as nearly-normal, not-too-weird, almost-ordinary occurrences when one is facing grief and loss. My logical mind could have comfortably catalogued the new experiences and then proceeded merrily along its logical way.

But that was not to be. The morning after he died, Dad tapped me on the shoulder as I did my morning jog, stood before me looking like a radiant almost-human mist, and spoke to me with such intense tenderness and power that all previous understanding of those states paled instantly by comparison. On the morning after his death, my father's spirit launched me suddenly and unexpectedly on my spiritual journey.

Nothing was the same for me from that moment forward. In one split second I dropped my identity as an agnostic, recognized that I am more than just a body and a logical mind, and began profuse apologies to all the older women I had maligned for their infatuation with dead people. On that morning I instantly became either a New Age seeker or an old-fashioned mystic—or both.

On the morning after he died, my father gave me the gift of the Light, and one glimpse of its radiance left me with very little choice. I was hooked. Those few tender seconds with my father changed my life forever.

~ ~ ~

It was ten months after Dad's death when I met Osirin. He introduced himself to me during a deep meditation in which I had asked to meet my spirit guide or heavenly guru. I had asked for guidance, but when Osirin began to speak in my mind, I wasn't entirely sure that I wanted to open myself to his presence. It seems easier for fleshly beings like me to accept the presence and comradeship of a disincarnate soul when that disembodied being is someone previously known in earth life. But what about a stranger? I was taught as a child never to accept candy from a stranger. What about a *really strange stranger*, one with no body, offering not just sweets, but wisdom and love? No one had ever taught me what to do in a situation like that.

My heart was enamored of Osirin from our first meeting, but my logical mind was neither enamored nor humored by this disembodied soul. For weeks I was torn between what I felt was true, what I knew was supposed to be true, and what my mind told me surely had to be true. My resistance gradually weakened, however, and slowly I opened my ears to Osirin in spite of my logical mind's best efforts to discredit my experiences and doubt my sanity.

In current parlance Osirin would be called my spirit guide, although more often I think of him as my beloved friend, constant companion, and God-sent teacher. Osirin likes to write, and from our first meeting he has chosen the pen as his preferred teaching tool. Often as I meditate he instructs me gently, "A pen, please, little one." Osirin writes poems and stories, explaining to me whatever he wishes me to know. He patiently endures my confusion and resistance as we have long conversations on topics of his choice or mine. He answers the questions I ask, often in depth far beyond my expectation or comprehension, and he uses my curiosity to nudge me into realms of learning I never would have explored alone. I talk with him, banter with him, even struggle with him as I ask that he guide me and lead me toward the Light of God.

I'm quite sure as I look back over my life that Osirin has been with me every step of the way, but I did not meet him until ten months after Dad died. During those ten months I meditated, prayed, read, and struggled in all the ways I could think of— some helpful, some not, some graceful, some clumsy. Osirin did not spring into my life unexpectedly the way my Dad's spirit did. I worked very hard to pave the way for him to be able to reach me, and finally he did.

Sometimes I still wonder exactly who Osirin is. He may be a heavenly messenger. He may be an ambassador from God sent specifically to teach me. He may be a friend from my distant past with whom I shared earthly pleasures and earthly treasures a few thousand years ago. He may be a master guide, an oversoul, or an enlightened master. Or he may be me—whatever that means and however that works. He may be a part of my soul, my higher self, or my still-quiet-voice-within. He may be the voice of the God spark within the inner chambers of my heart. As long as I walk this earth in a physical body and must, by design, pay homage to my logical, physical mind, I doubt I will "know" exactly who Osirin is. On most days, however, I'm content with not knowing as love usually needs no name and wisdom needs no ID.

Over the three years that I have been aware of Osirin's presence, many pages have rolled out of my computer printer. My early conversations with Osirin, as well as many of his words and lessons to me, were written in my first book, *Stardust*. Now as I write *On The Wings of Spirit*, it is his hand that leads me. The lessons shared in this book are transcripts of conversations and intimate moments with Osirin. I offer these words and lessons to you, dear reader, as a gift. And I ask a gift in return. As you read, remember that the only path I can walk is the one beneath my feet, and the only path you can walk is the one beneath your feet. All of us who quest search for wisdom and peace, yet each path is unique. As you read of my journey, pause often to pay homage to the richness of your own.

It is my hope that the lessons I have learned along my path will prove useful to you and that the words that have healed many aches in my heart might gently touch your heart as well.

CHAPTER ONE

A LESSON ON LETTING GO

Most journeyers do not have as dramatic an introduction to their spiritual quests as I did. Many seekers find their way onto the path quietly and slowly. Some begin their journeys in their dream worlds, some find themselves gently nudged by art or music, some find a crack in the door through their experiences of parenting or loving. More than a few have felt the gentle arms of Spirit at a church altar, on a mountain peak, or beneath a setting sun. These patient seekers open their hearts to Spirit bit by bit, growing gracefully in their own rhythm and time.

Perhaps this is my romanticized illusion and, in fact, there is no slow and graceful path at all. Or perhaps it was simply not my lot to travel such a path. When someone stumbles upon the Big Bang initiation into spiritual awareness as I did, that initiation often centers around a near-death experience or the death of a loved one. Death is quite a powerful teacher. When my Dad died, I had no idea that there was such a thing as a Big Bang. I planned to do my grieving the way the psychological cookbooks outlined, for those recipes are tried and true. I knew what to expect, how to cope, when to cry, and where to turn for help. I had an excellent strategy planned, but it got blown to smithereens by the Big Bang. When my Dad tapped me on the shoulder the morning after his death, coping went out the window and transformation rushed in. The power of the Big Bang won me over instantly, and I was willing to go wherever this marvelous energy cared to lead me.

For two years I followed the energy, apprenticed myself to Osirin, and entered into the lessons he brought to me. During those years Osirin taught me patiently and lovingly, initiating me into an entirely new way of understanding myself, my emotions, and my world. As a psychologist I worked every day with myself and my clients around issues of trust, loneliness, abandonment, fear, courage, and despair. I thought I knew quite well how those feelings are woven into the fabric of human experiences. Osirin gently showed me, however, that I had been living for years on the very small tip of a very large iceberg. He taught me, for example, that trust is not only an emotion and a psychological process; it is also the primary and essential fuel that propels a seeker along his spiritual highway. He showed me that despair is not only a feeling or the hallmark of a lousy mood; it is the proverbial bushel basket hiding the light of the soul. He showed me that rejection and abandonment, those beasts that torment every human psyche, are spiritually nonexistent. He taught me through his gentle commentaries and explanations of my everyday experiences. He taught me by his presence and his love.

The first phase of my spiritual journey ended as I wrote *Stardust*, describing my path, my lessons, my successes, and my failures of those two years. I cannot remember how long I rested at the end of Phase 1, but in cosmic time it was probably somewhat less than half an eyeblink. Phase 2 of my spiritual journey commenced on my thirty-seventh birthday. On that day I walked along the beach with the wide eyed blindness and innocent exuberance of a child. "In numerology three is a very magic number," I thought as I walked the beach, "and seven is a magic number. Together they make ten which is also a magic number. Thirty-seven is going to be a very special year for me."

My eyes found a particularly appealing cloud in the sky, and I imagined that cloud to be the face of Jesus. I looked into his eyes and said, "I'm ready for thirty-seven."

Almost instantly I heard a voice reply, "It is time to learn power and freedom."

"Super," I said as I skipped along the sand. "Power and freedom. What a wonderful birthday present! That sounds great. I'm ready."

The voice from the clouds asked soberly, "Are you sure?"

It is lucky that I possessed the innocent enthusiasm of a three-year-old on that day. Had I been logical, rational, and maturely thirty-seven, I would have politely asked Jesus to draft a formal proposal which I would carefully consider before deciding whether or not I was, in fact, ready. That's not what I did. I skipped with even more gusto on the sand and said, "Yes. I'm ready! I'm ready for power and freedom."

And so the die was cast. It was promised long ago that if we ask, we shall receive. It was not promised that the process of receiving shall always delight the earthly ego. Very often when I ask for gifts from Spirit, the gifts come wrapped in packages that I do not initially understand and, in some cases, do not like. Consequently, I was quite distressed when the course description for my first class in The University of Power and Freedom was delivered a few days later. I heard Osirin's voice in my mind saying repeatedly, "Little one, it is time to release the nursery."

The nursery was a business I had begun seven years earlier. It had been a consuming labor of love for me and several other people. We had collected scores of unique plants, learned to propagate them, displayed them in our well-tended gardens, educated gardeners on their use, and modestly considered ourselves junior pioneers in the nursery industry. Now I was being told to let it go.

I resisted this directive vigorously, although from the start I knew somewhere inside myself that my protests were nothing more than stalling tactics. There are many things I would do the moment Spirit asks, but in this case I could not see how to gracefully and quickly release four employees, one hundred thousand plants, and twenty-two acres of land. How could I turn my back on all the love and labor that had been poured into the land, I wondered. This course requirement made no sense to me, and I considered dropping out of the university altogether. Instead of resigning in a fit of fury, however, I turned often to Osirin and asked for help.

"Osirin, please help me," I implored. "I don't understand. You know that I trust you, but I don't understand why this is being asked of me."

"Take my hand, little one," Osirin gently began. "Let's walk together. Imagine that we are walking home, perhaps through a thick forest with unfamiliar trails and areas of dense undergrowth. Take out your scythe and I'll take out mine. Let's cut away the brush so that we can move forward. Stop—do you hear the song of that bird? Cut more. Stop—do you feel the caress of the breeze? Cut more. Stop—do you feel me by your side? Do you hear the sound of my scythe as it clears the path ahead of you?

"Little one, this journey called humanness is one of the most exciting adventures in the universe. Throughout all time and all space, there are very few adventures available to a soul that are as challenging or as noble as entering a body. I applaud you, little one, for your valor."

"Valor?" I asked with surprise. "I don't feel particularly courageous right now, and I hardly deserve any spiritual applause."

"You have made your way deep into the forest of humanness," Osirin continued. "You have traveled far into the woods of your life."

"Maybe so, Osirin," I replied, "but only with lots and lots of help from you. I couldn't have done any of it without you, and I can't proceed one inch further without your help. I'm very confused about the nursery."

"You never have to travel without me, little one. That is a given. No man travels alone. No forest is uninhabited. No jungle is without guides who know its secrets and its treasures.

"You are entering a new forest, or I might as accurately say you are traveling much deeper into a very familiar forest. The forest of power and freedom is not unlike a majestic redwood grove where trees that have stood for a thousand years hold within them centuries of knowledge and wisdom and roots that penetrate into decades of rich, dark earth. This forest will frighten you at times, little one. You must begin to release the nursery, and this is both frightening and confusing. We must begin our journey slowly, even tediously."

"How will I be frightened on this path?" I asked with apprehension.

"Relax, little one. Have my words made you afraid?"

"No, not really," I said. "I trust you deeply, Osirin. I just wish I knew what to expect."

"Expect adventure, little one! I have my scythe in hand. Grab yours. Now, let's go."

~ ~ ~

A few days later I asked, "Osirin, I'm still very confused about this lesson. Did you answer my questions about the nursery?"

"Not exactly," he teased, "but you must admit that I gave you a rather nice introduction."

"Yes, you did," I agreed. "It was a lovely introduction. Will you help me more with my pain and confusion?"

"All things change," Osirin began. "I've told you that many times and in many ways. The nursery was a creation of beauty and love. As such it has served your growth well over the past seven years. Now new lessons are to be learned and new roads are to be traveled."

"Why does something of beauty have to be destroyed?" I asked. "It doesn't make sense to me."

"Little one," Osirin asked, "was your father destroyed by his death?"

"No," I said. "Oh, I think I see. No, he wasn't destroyed at all. When I saw him the morning after his death he seemed radiant and purified, not dead at all."

"Then why do you believe that the nursery can die?"

"Well," I said in a state of increasing confusion, "that's different."

"To you it appears to be different," Osirin replied.

"Osirin, isn't it different?"

"Nothing of love ever dies," Osirin gently said.

"I can almost understand that when we are talking about people, but when it comes to a business, I don't get the point."

"Then trust. Simply trust. Remember that goodbye does not mean loss. An ending is not a destruction. Love and beauty are energies that live on and on. Once you give them birth, you literally cannot destroy them."

5

Osirin's words brought a deep sense of relaxation. "What a beautiful thought," I said. "What a blessed relief!"

"Now, little one," he said, "rest in your relief and in your belief. And prepare for hard work."

~ ~ ~

Disembodied teachers are no different in some ways from those with bodies. Each teacher is unique; each has his or her own special gifts to give. Osirin is a poet, a storyteller, a dreamer, and a coach. But he is most definitely not a businessman. When Osirin made it clear that I was to begin preparations to release the nursery, he introduced me to a new teacher whose name, Sophorel, seemed to indicate that he possessed wisdom, and I certainly needed a heavy dose of just that.

During the months that followed, Sophorel appeared regularly in my meditations holding a red notebook in his hands. He never spoke. If I relaxed deeply enough and trusted fully enough I could see words written on the pages of the red notebook. I transcribed the words, and in this manner Sophorel gave me directions on how to proceed with this difficult project.

Sophorel directed me to reorganize our production techniques at the nursery, to inventory and re-inventory all the thousands of plants, to change our sales strategies one after another, and to make plans for large clearance sales. There were at least three major phases of reorganization that Sophorel directed over a twelve-month period, each phase leading to a smaller, simpler business. At many points along the way I chose to believe that the goal was not to end the nursery, but to simplify it to the point that it would demand less of my energy, freeing me to spend more time studying, writing, and journeying. Spirit often speaks in symbols and metaphors, so I tried to convince myself that "releasing" the nursery was a lesson in simplifying a cumbersome business rather than ending it.

Many hours in front of the computer and much more physical labor than I was prepared for were required of me during the lengthy process. I longed for a rest, but whenever I pleaded for time off, I would find words in Sophorel's red book telling me

I needed to work, not rest. I turned to Osirin, imploring him to bring me soft meditations, sweet poems, or gentle reassurances. Usually he would comply with my wishes, but each poem would end with the words, "Now go to the nursery and get to work."

During the months that Osirin and Sophorel directed me to release the nursery, I could see no farther down the spiritual path than my shoelaces. I was confused, exhausted, and lonely as my work progressed. I pleaded often with Osirin and Sophorel to make the lesson easier, clear, or faster. Sophorel answered my pleas, explaining that releasing the nursery was a complex and lengthy exercise, a necessary step in the lesson of power. Releasing the nursery was not guaranteed to endow me with power, but he taught me that I must practice the exercises given to me in order to strengthen my power muscles. Otherwise, I would never pass the course. The words in Sophorel's red notebook said: "The nursery is only one part of this lesson upon which you embark. This year you will learn the lesson of the nursery, yet deep within it lies the lesson of power. This is a rather long lesson, and the answers will be not be immediately forthcoming. The power that you must learn is different from power you have known before, just as the trust Osirin taught you years ago is different from the trust you knew before. This is a hard lesson, so prepare yourself for the challenges of this new year. I will instruct you regarding the nursery. Be aware that solutions to problems at the nursery are a part, a very small part, of the quest for power. Do not be misguided that in solving the problems of the nursery you will learn power. You will not. However, I will guide you in that way, for you must solve these problems as exercises in your search for power."

It was more than a year before I fully accepted and implemented the mandate on the nursery. Finally, I was ready to let it go in whatever way that process might unfold. I was ready to sell it, rent it, or close the gates and walk away if that was required of me. When I finally surrendered and followed Sophorel's orders to the letter, my struggles lightened almost instantly. As I let go of my resistance, much of the stress on me and my employees at the nursery lifted, bad luck turned into good luck, and our spirits softened. We announced that the nursery would be closing and began an exhausting but speedy process of selling all the plants we had collected and tended over the years. Spirit was clearly with us in many ways during the final months, and as the end approached our hearts were light rather than filled with the pain we had all anticipated.

Twenty months after my thirty-seventh birthday, together with my dear friend who had been manager of the nursery for those seven years, I closed the gates for the last time and our dream came to a gentle end. As I drove away from the nursery that day, I heard Osirin's voice: ''Remember that all life is a process of taking in and releasing. Just as you must inhale and exhale to live, you must practice the gentle and graceful acceptance of both receiving and letting go in all parts of your life. That which you release is not destroyed. As you exhale, the air that you release is taken up by other forms of life. It is the same in all things that you release with love. There is no way to know power or freedom until you know the gift of release, the beauty of letting go, the liberation of goodbye. A person of power travels lightly through life, ready to release what is no longer helpful or that which is needed elsewhere in the universe. Feel your sadness, little one, but also notice that tucked quietly beneath your sadness is a different emotion—it is the sweetness of freedom, the freedom that comes with a trusting and loving goodbye.''

CHAPTER TWO

LOST IN THE SKIES AND
NOWHERE TO TURN

I had been enrolled in The University of Power and Freedom for only a few months when it became clear to me that releasing nurseries was not the only skill taught or learned within its hallowed halls. I noticed that many of my friends and clients were students in the same esteemed institution of higher learning, yet their courses were quite different from mine. Osirin assured me that my studies were designed to meet my needs and to diminish my personal deficiencies. This university, he often reminded me, had not been founded for me alone; it is open to any and all who wish to enroll.

I was so thoroughly engrossed in my work at the nursery that I was surprised when I found a second course card from the university in my mental mailbox. I was so surprised, in fact, that I ignored it. It made its way again into my mailbox, so finally I read the course description. It said: *It's time to learn to fly.* Lovely metaphor, I presumed, and tossed it into my mental trashcan—that overstuffed receptacle in my brain which holds unhelpful notions, wacky emotions, dumb ideas, and outdated theories.

When I began to feel an overwhelming desire to learn to fly, I assumed I had simply lost my mind. I also assumed, giving myself the benefit of the doubt, that the insanity was temporary and would soon pass. I tried to ignore the persistent thoughts of airplanes soaring through my mind and dismissed the accompanying rapturous feelings as some type of esoteric symbolism which would surely subside.

The desire to fly grew stronger. Images of airplanes appeared in my meditations and eagles began to soar in my dreams. For six months I resisted. After all, I was entirely too busy following Sophorel's orders at the nursery to read about flying or inquire about instruction. I did, however, ask Osirin what my flights of fantasy were about.

"Osirin," I inquired, "did you put these thoughts into my head for some reason or am I simply crazy? What's going on between me and airplanes?"

As usual, Osirin answered me. His words came strongly and clearly as though he had been itching for months, maybe centuries, to push me from an earthbound nest into the sky. "Little one," he said, "as truly as you believe in me and in God you must struggle against your fear of freedom, against your fear of flying free. As a boat sails, it cannot doubt the wind. As a bird soars, it cannot doubt its wings. As a woman flies, she cannot doubt her freedom. Your fantasy of becoming a pilot is quite timely. Trust it. The essence of your wish to pilot an airplane is the wish for freedom. When you fly an airplane, you are not free from the ground; you are free within the air. You are free within, not from, and this is true freedom. Freedom is having the wings of the angel within. Let your wings develop such strength that they will hold you aloft. Your wings are weak from years of unuse and abuse. Courage will heal your wings. You do not yet understand. In time you will see. Embrace your fear of flying free. Fly, little one. Fly!"

Osirin was right—I did not yet understand. I did not see the connection between the study of aerodynamics and spiritual growth. I couldn't see how sitting behind a propeller would teach me freedom. Nevertheless, the desire within me steadily grew, so I called the local airport and scheduled my first lesson in the sky.

The very first time I flew, it was clear to me that I was not a "born pilot." It took many weeks of study before I could consistently remember the difference between an aileron and a rudder, and it took months before I could feel in my bones when the airplane was ready to lift off the ground and when it was ready to settle back to earth for a landing. There was nothing natural to me about flying, and there was probably nothing on earth more alien to me than concepts such as lead buildup on spark plugs, carburetor icing, and overly rich fuel mixtures. Nevertheless, I flew, and soon I knew that I wouldn't stop. I still saw very little connection between spiritual power and the horsepower generated by the Lycoming engine that lifted me into the skies, but I flew nonetheless, often feeling an odd mixture of terror, exhiliaration, peace, and chaos as I soared with an instructor beside me.

When the time came for my first solo flight, I knew I was crossing an important spiritual threshold—one I could neither clearly verbalize nor discuss with my instructor, as I sensed he would not share my perspective. As he climbed out of the airplane and said, "Take it around three times," I taxied away clutching the bear claw that hung secretly near by solar plexus and praying for courage and safety. The symbolism of the experience was striking. I sat alone in a machine that generated more power than I could comfortably manage, power which could either kill me or lift me higher than I could otherwise go. Soon I would lift high into the ethers where no earthling but myself would sit at the controls of my destiny. Fear, courage, and curiosity blended into one energy as I advanced the throttle and lifted off the ground.

Flying alone that day was an adventure in contradictions. I felt both terrified and courageous, free within the sky and vulnerable within my tiny airplane, master of my fate and potential victim of nature's slightest whim. On that day I could not clearly tell the difference between power and fear, between freedom and terror. I couldn't tell the difference, and I knew I needed to learn.

∿　　∿　　∿

Several weeks later as I planted seven new azaleas in my woodland garden, I noticed that the wind whipped more briskly than usual in the trees over my head. Gusty days are delightful to gardeners, and I enjoyed the breeze until I remembered that I was scheduled to fly at 3 o'clock. Gusty days are not so delightful to student pilots. When the man at the weather service station told me that the wind was 10 knots on the ground and 35 knots at 3,000 feet aloft, I felt very ambivalent about departing terra firma. Why should I want to get blown around like a child's balloon or a toy rocket? Ten knots of crosswind is a gentle breeze to an experienced pilot, but it might as well have been Hurricane Hilda as far as I was concerned. Why not don my work gloves, grab my shovel, and return to my garden? Why should I give in to this strong urge to fly on such a windy day?

I drove to the airport and caught my instructor between lessons. "Are you free now?" I asked him.

"Maybe," he said. "Are you going to fly?"

"I assumed you wouldn't let me fly alone," I answered. "The wind worries me a little."

"I know," he said. "It's brisk in spots, but you can handle it. You can fly to Burlington if you want."

"Will you fly with me?" I asked. "The last time I flew alone the alternator went out, I drained the battery, the radios died, and the fuel gauges read an inaccurate but alarming *empty*. I was emotionally equipped for a challenge that day, but not today. Will you fly with me?"

"I'll see," he said. "You preflight the plane and I'll see if my next student shows up."

Most flight instructors have the ability to appear serenely calm when ordinary mortals would tear their hair and gnash their teeth. Adopting a pose of casual and unflappable bliss while students panic is one of their trademarks. This particular flight instructor was the cream of the calm crop. I failed to appreciate his apparent inner peace as my stomach grew tighter and my legs began to tremble.

"OK," I said. "I'll preflight the plane. Then I'll cruise by here and pick you up. Just hop in when I taxi by."

I slipped the key to Cessna 69195 into my pocket, walked slowly to the airplane, and began the preflight check. Yep, wings are still attached. Is my instructor coming? Landing gear intact. Is he coming? Why am I so jumpy? Yep, fuel is free of water bubbles. No hornets have nested in the pitot tube, the oil is above

5 quarts, and the propeller appears to be firmly hooked onto the front of the airplane. *Is he coming?*

I started the engine and slowly taxied toward the runway hoping he would appear out of nowhere and hop in. He didn't. "To hell with it," I thought. "I can fly this thing without him. Who needs him!" Defiance and bravado are almost always signs of impending trouble, especially when accompanied by sweaty palms. I should have known better.

"Chapel Hill traffic, Cessna 69195 is departing runway 26," I said into the mike, and off I flew.

Burlington is a half hour's drive from Chapel Hill. To get there you take Highway 54 until it hits Interstate 85. You turn left on I-85 and, voilá, there's Burlington. That's exactly how you fly it, too, if you fly the way a student pilot should fly. The route of the novice is to fly a few miles east of Highway 54 to I-85, turn left about 5 miles before the interstate, and look for the airport. Simple. Nobody in her right mind can get lost between Chapel Hill and Burlington no matter whether she is on the ground or above the ground.

I flew to Burlington and practiced a few landings. As I headed home, I decided to fly my compass instead of the interstate, putting my novice navigational skills to a premature test. On the way home I practiced a few maneuvers which took my mind and my eyes off the ground. When I put my nose down and looked around, I didn't recognize anything. Undaunted, I flew on. Chapel Hill had to be nearby.

Five minutes after I should have been near Chapel Hill, I started to feel unsettled. I recognized absolutely nothing on the ground. I was a very green aviator, so I performed one of the few intelligent moves available to me given my scant hours as pilot-in-command. I made a 180-degree turn. In my growing confusion I concluded that if I knew exactly where I had come from and by exactly what course, I could turn around, fly the reciprocal course, and return to home base. What I forgot was the wind. I forgot that I was no different to those 35 knots of moving air than if I had been a tiny seedpod from a giant maple tree.

As I attempted to return to Burlington I was being blown far off course by the wind, although I still did not realize it. I struggled to get the appropriate map out of my flight bag, but I soon gave up on its ability to help me. By that time I was disoriented and had lost all confidence in my sense of direction. I tried to tune in the onboard VOR (very-high-frequency omnidirectional range) navigational equipment, but in my confusion I could not remember how to set it on a homeward course. When I realized that I was incompetent to make use of my equipment, I felt a coldness running through my body that was terrifying.

My thoughts turned suddenly to my father, who had been a pilot before he died. Only a few months earlier I had inherited his logbooks, records of all his hours in the sky. In those records I could see times he had come to visit me and trips we had taken together. I could also see the fateful point at which his brain cancer had been diagnosed, for beyond that day he logged the few hours remaining to him as pilot-second-in-command and never as pilot-in-command. In an intimate moment between us, I gazed at my father's last photograph and totaled the columns on the last page of his logbook. I finished one small and perhaps totally inconsequential piece of his earthly business, but I felt deep pride and sorrow in being the first person on this earth to know that Dad flew exactly 1,090.6 hours before he died.

I looked below me. There were only farms and fields. No towns were to be seen. The world looks mighty barren and empty when you're lost in the sky. Overpopulation seems to be a hoax when you need a town and can't find one.

Corn fields began to look inviting, although I knew the hidden surprises they hold for a small airplane landing in distress. I checked my fuel. Plenty remained. The skies, although increasingly hazy, offered at least five miles of visibility, and I knew I could fly on if only I could control my growing sense of panic. I flew northwest for a few minutes, then west, then in circles. Soon I had no idea where I had come from, where I was headed, or what to do. Nothing made sense and nothing was familiar. I was thoroughly lost.

The blood ran cold through my body and I began to feel sick. I had tried everything I knew to try. I had even experimented with many things the pilots' training books say not to do, including flying in random directions and flying closer and closer to the ground seeking a false and risky sense of security close to the bosom of Mother Earth. I had tried it all. I had nothing left to do. So I screamed. I looked over the nose of my Cessna and yelled into the skies at the top of my lungs, "I'm lost! I'm really lost and I'm very scared. Please help me!"

I then heard a familiar voice. It was not Osirin, it was not Sophorel, and it was not my Guardian Angel. I heard Dad say from the copilot's seat, "Fly north." In my anxiety, I argued with him saying, "I don't think so, Dad. That will just make things worse. I should be flying northwest or maybe west, not north. Please help me, but don't make things worse."

Dad's voice was insistent and stern, just the way it sometimes sounded when I was a child. *"Fly north,"* he repeated. Who was I to argue further? I was a lost novice pilot and he was a veteran multi-engine and instrument-rated pilot with the definite advantage of a celestial perspective. I banked right until the heading indicator read 000, and that's as due north as any little Cessna can fly.

Even though I was flying with divine guidance, I was still scared. Flying with an invisible copilot provided me a bit of comfort, but it did not put an end to the trembling sensation that raced through my body. I had little faith in my ability to gain any assistance from the radio, but I picked up my mike and tried calling Burlington.

"Burlington Unicom, this is 69195, do you read me?"

I heard a faint "we read you" over the radio.

"Burlington, I'm lost."

Burlington responded very quickly, telling me to call one-crackle-nine-static-garble.

"Burlington, please repeat," I said. "I can't understand you."

Once again I was told to contact one-one-garble-point-noise.

"Burlington, I still can't hear you. I don't know how far away I am, but I can't make out what you're telling me to do."

Finally I got it. I was to tune my radio to 119.1. I did. But who is 119.1, I wondered? Is it God's frequency? Osirin's channel? Probably neither.

I called the spirit of 119.1. "This is Cessna 69195. Do you read me?"

15

"69195, I read you," a voice replied.

"I'm a student pilot," I said, probably in a rather pitiful voice. "I don't know who you are or how you can help me. I'm lost. That's all I know. I'm lost."

To a student pilot, most radio chatter sounds more like Chinese than English, and ears that ring with increasing panic do not help the matter. I understood enough of what the controller said to know that he was very concerned and was trying to help me. Frequently I heard the controller say my call number, Cessna 69195; after that, however, all his words were garbled and far more distracting than helpful. Realizing that communication with people on the ground was futile and ineffective, I began looking again at the fields below me, wishing desperately that one would magically transform itself into a runway or perhaps rise to cradle me very gently in its green arms.

I was about to give up and turn off the radio, preferring silence to deafening static and unintelligible chatter, when I saw a cluster of buildings ahead of me. "Wait a minute," I said to my unidentified friend on 119.1, "I think I see a city." I flew due east fearing that the visions below were a mirage. I assumed that desperate pilots must surely imagine cities like sunbaked nomads imagine palm trees in the desert. I expected my imaginary city to disappear as I flew closer through the haze.

"Wait a minute again! I think I see an airport!" I said excitedly into my mike. I imagine those words lowered the blood pressure of many air traffic controllers, pilots, and worried folks on the ground in Chapel Hill who were, unbeknownst to me, eavesdropping on my crisis.

I recognized the numbers on the ends of the runways. A very friendly 6 and a deeply appreciated 9 were painted in huge white numbers on the ends of the two runways ahead of me. I had never approached Burlington from the west, but I had landed often on that very 6 and that very 9, so I knew I was found. I realized, soberly and gratefully, that if I had flown west/northwest as I had initially insisted to Dad, I would have been lost for another hour or I would have unknowingly competed for airspace with jets as they landed at Greensboro. Or Dad and I would have flown together, sans bodies, into sunsets and stardust and moonlight. But now I was safe. I knew where I was. I found the interstate and flew it home.

~   ~   ~

Becca: Osirin, I'm scared to fly again. I'm not sure I can ever do it again.

Osirin: You have two choices, little one. You can study and learn, or you can give up.

Becca: I'll study. But what is the lesson? Why did this happen? Why did I get lost?

Osirin: It's a metaphor, little one. It's a metaphor for life.

Becca: I nearly crash and burn and you call it a metaphor?!

Osirin: Slow down, little one. What would you call it?

Becca: Terror, that's what.

Osirin: Terror of what?

Becca: Terror of . . . of terror.

Osirin: Go on.

Becca: It's the fear that was horrible.

Osirin: And being lost?

Becca: That wasn't so bad. It's the fear that was crippling.

Osirin: Yes, little one.

Becca: Osirin, what is the lesson?

Osirin: You adventured into the skies on a flight into the beyond. When you feared you were lost, you consulted all your earthly guides and found none to be useful. Then you screamed. Your scream may have saved you. The kind people on the radio are your friends, the maps are your guides, and the navigation aids are your leaders. But only God can save you. It is only God who has ever saved you. God's voice may come from me, from your father, from your soul, or from your next door neighbor. When you hear God's voice, it is love which speaks, and his love is your salvation. *If you fly with his love, there is nothing to fear and nothing other than his love to need.* We shall call this lesson "lost in the skies and nowhere to turn." Do you like it?

Becca: It's catchy, Osirin. I like it. So you are telling me that the lesson here is fear?

Osirin: In part. The lesson is also on the erroneous belief that you ever navigate alone and on the erroneous belief that you are ever lost.

Becca: Oh, I see.

Osirin: You're never alone, little one. Never. So why should you fear?

Becca: Thank you, Osirin. Thank you.

~ ~ ~

It is very hard for me as I walk this earth to remember that I am not alone. My crisis in the sky was a poignantly dangerous experience in the terror of utter aloneness—total disconnection from home, earth, safety, and all of mankind. It was like a nightmare come true, like a karmic or mythic archetype of horror enacted at 3,500 feet above the earth. The terror of being utterly and completely alone was so strong that it possibly would have killed me in a few more minutes. But I wasn't alone. My Dad was there. Not metaphorically or symbolically there—*he was literally with me.*

Without Dad's help that day I might have died, but that fact seemed oddly irrelevant to me as I thought about the deeper meanings within my crisis. Dad said, "Fly north," and those two words perhaps kept me alive, but later as I studied this lesson I realized he had said far more than that. He might as well have said to me: "I can tell you where to fly, but you must do the flying. I'm with you, truly with you, but you must exercise your own power and courage. I am with you, but you are the pilot."

The fear of separateness, isolation, and abandonment seems to be part of the basic package we humans bring with us into physical life. I have never known a person who dug to the bottom of her inner pit and did not discover her unique version of that fear hidden somewhere underneath the many protective layers of personality and ego. By virtue of these bodies we inhabit and these five senses that define what we "know," it appears to us humans that we can, indeed, be alone. We seem to be separate and apart from each other, from the Tao, from the flow, from God. I felt the full power of that illusion at 3,500 feet.

18

In the months since I was lost in the sky and on each and every flight since that time, I pause before starting the engine, look upward, and say these words aloud if I'm by myself and silently if an instructor or a passenger might misunderstand: "I fly in the arms of your love, dear God, for there is nowhere else to fly." I ask my father to sit in the co-pilot's seat and Osirin to sit in the back, and I invoke the spirit of the little pewter eagle who always flies with me, asking her to teach me her power in the sky. I never fly alone any more. Never.

Slowly, very slowly, I am digesting the wisdom within this lesson one bit at a time, one iota after another iota. Perhaps someday I will fully know, believe, trust, and live as though I am neither alone nor powerless—not in the sky, not on the ground, and not deep within myself. I am never forgotten by the spirit who was my earthly father or by the Spirit who has always been my Divine Father. I am not without love—ever. In Truth, I am never lost, never powerless, and never alone.

CHAPTER THREE

LESSONS ON RELATIONSHIPS

Every semester The University of Power and Freedom publishes a student handbook which lists all the courses that are taught behind its invisible walls. Simultaneously the U. of P.& F. distributes course cards to its students. At best, these cards serve as invitations to learning. At worst, they are reminders of karma to be cleansed, psychic trashpiles to be disposed of, and spiritual requirements yet to be fulfilled. I was already enrolled in P&F 101 *(The Basics of Nursery Releasing)* and P&F 203 *(Be More Grounded—Learn to Fly)*. I assumed I was taking a full load and that no more would be required of me for a while. I was wrong. Releasing nurseries and flying airplanes are tough things to learn. Tougher still, and far more distressing, was the third course card I found in my mental mailbox: Power and Freedom 305—*Self-Clarification Through Advanced Marital Pain*.

My husband, Victor, and I had been through hard times before and had, I thought, mastered them. Consequently, the severity of our troubles surprised me. Since Victor and I are both psychologists, we had spent a great deal of time working on ourselves and our relationship. Few plumbers would live for years with a stopped-up toilet, few roofers would live for years with water dripping into the den, and few psychologists live for years with unattended emotional pain. We attended to the pain in all the ways we could, but the pain proved to be bigger than our best efforts and we separated for a while.

Since my spiritual quest began, Osirin has talked to me often about love. According to everything I read and everything I am told by Osirin, love is not merely the goal we journeyers devotedly seek; it is, enigmatically, the only thing that is. Love, it seems, is the Alpha, the Omega, and everything in between.

I have known since the day after my father's death that love is the foundation upon which the rest of my journey would be built, for on that morning my father appeared in a mist that to my suddenly opened eyes was clearly composed of different hues and various densities of love. I knew on that morning, and I know just as clearly today, that my father's spirit not only spoke to me of love and not only infused me with a nearly electrifying shot of love, but was actually made of divine love.

In those brief moments with Dad I knew divine love to be a feeling, an essence, a state of creating, a quality of both matter and non-matter, an energy in constant motion and a dynamically unending stasis. In the course of my everyday existence, however, my eyes are not so clear and I rarely find myself plugged directly into the spiritual socket of total wisdom. Consequently, I often wrinkle my brow and wonder how on earth Osirin expects me to manifest divine love within this coarse material plane and how it is that we humans can hope to perform divine dances with each other while seriously encumbered with bodies, egos, personalities, needs, wants, pains, histories, futures, and logic.

Human love has admittedly brought me many moments of precious tenderness and near bliss, but there have been many other moments during my life when human love has felt to me like an albatross hanging heavily over my heart chakra. Being in a loving relationship—whether that be with my husband, my clients, my son, my siblings, my colleagues, or my friends— sometimes feels like a burden too great to bear, a lesson too difficult to learn, and an exam that forebodes only failure. Bridging the enormous gap that I discovered in my life between divine love and human love and struggling to find the common ground between the two became a consuming quest for me during and after the months of our marital separation. I knew that understanding more about the weaving of divine love into my human relationships is a crucial part of my training in The University of Power and Freedom, but for months all I felt was fear, confusion, and bondage to my ignorance. Osirin taught me patiently and gently, yet with a slight sense of urgency. His lessons came much faster than I could absorb them, but I dutifully transcribed the words he gave me and studied them a pace slower than the pace at which he taught. Osirin began his lessons on love with a fairy tale:

"Little one, I want to talk with you about the struggle that you experience in your relationships. This may seem a bit lengthy and circuitous, but I shall begin with a story.

"Once there was a young maiden named Mary. She lived in a deep, dark forest far from the light of the sun. As she grew she became more and more beautiful, but none could see her beauty in the darkness of the forest. Far away lived a gallant young warrior named Mark. He lived in a dark cave and, like Mary, was also a stranger to the light.

"One day Mary ventured into the forest in search of her heart's mate. She had felt him beckoning to her in her dreams, though they had never met. She traveled to find him, thinking that surely he must live nearby. Mary traveled so far that she began to see the rays of the sun. She mistook these rays of light for danger and recoiled from them, hiding in terror beneath branches and leaves, her face buried into the darkness of the ground.

"Meanwhile, Mark had ventured forth from his cave to seek his soul's mate who had also appeared in his dreams. As he entered into the light of the sun, he mistook the rays of light for fire from the mouth of a dragon and attempted to slay the light with his sword.

"So familiar were the two lovers with the darkness of their youth that they misunderstood the light which would bring them together. Mary hid in fear until her beauty was lost, and Mark fought valiantly against the sun until his courage and valor eroded into despair. Their love remained forever a dream they dreamed in the dark.

"Now, little one, take a moment to let this story settle within you. Feel the sacrifice that the lovers made. You and many others of your time misunderstand the light. You fail to see its kindness and gentleness, and you run from it or attempt to slay it.

"The darkness of this story, little one, is the ego. In your culture, you worship the ego more than it has ever before been worshipped. You adore your personalities more than man has

23

ever done, and you judge your fellow man more on the qualities of his personality and his ego than ever has been done in the history of man. You fall in love with personalities and egos, and this is the love of the darkness. When the light shines upon that love, threatening to shatter it, you hide in fear or you fight in anger against this unwelcomed intruder. The light is the light of genuine love and its glow is soft, little one. It cannot outshine the brilliant fireworks of a well-polished ego.

"The ego can always outshine the soul—at least for a moment or two. When its burst of fireworks is done and all its energy is spent, however, there is nothing left. The light of the soul is soft and gentle, little one. It is also eternal.

"Most of you in your culture fall in love with fireworks displays. Then when the sun begins to break through the night sky, which was the background for the fireworks, you are terrified. You run back to the night, trusting your ego as though surely it can produce genuine love. And on and on it goes. Beckon to the night, and it will return. But what happens to your beauty? No one can see it. What happens to your valor? It erodes slowly until you are a broken, despairing, embittered person."

The story of Mark and Mary poured out of my fingers and onto the computer screen in about ten minutes. It took at least twenty times that long to even begin to understand it. Osirin said that we humans, at least those of us in twentieth century Western civilization, usually fall in love with egos. We are trained from childhood to polish our egos, shine them up, mold them to the expectations of our subculture, and master the intricate sets of rules on how, when, and where to display our shiny wares. When we fall in love with another person we are usually mesmerized by certain qualities of the ego, while at the same time touched deeply, gently, and very quietly by the soul. Tragically, as the ego fails to keep us enchanted and entertained, we forget all about the soul of our beloved, and we turn away. A lot of what we call falling in love translates crassly into something like this: "I judge your personality as being an A+ " or "Your ego fills in the empty spots in my ego quite nicely." No personality is consistent and no ego is eternal, so love which is based on these tenuous pillars is bound to collapse in even the slightest earthquake.

When we love someone, there are two egos involved and two personalities dancing together, sometimes gracefully and sometimes like two clumsy boors. Beneath love's outer layers of delight, drama, and occasional despair, however, there are two souls. What about those two souls, I kept wondering. What about the souls beneath the personalities and the egos? When two adults fall in love, how do their souls love? How do they connect? How do they heal? How do they grow together? What about the souls?

∿   ∿   ∿

Osirin: Your job these days involves less time floating with angels and more time plowing in the fields. Not all meditation is performed in one's inner sky. Much of it is done in the fields under the hot sun. Labor hard, little one. Toil, struggle, and plow that someday these inner fields will be ripe with a rich harvest. Now I will tell you more about relationships. As you struggle with another person you often lose sight of the goal. When two egos struggle there is no sense of ultimate destiny, for no ego is concerned with destiny. Look up destiny.

Becca: I know the meaning of destiny, Osirin.

Osirin: Look it up anyway. Do definition number 2.

Becca: Okay. Destiny number 2 means "the preordained or inevitable course of events considered as something beyond the power or control of man: Marriage and hanging go by destiny."* Cute, Osirin. I particularly like the link between marriage and hanging. Very cute.

Osirin: Thank you, little one. Sometimes getting you to smile is not the easiest of tasks, but I persist and sometimes I succeed. Karma and dharma are not really so serious. Smile. Shall we go on?

Becca: Sure. I'm smiling and I'm ready.

*All definitions quoted throughout this book are from *The American Heritage Dictionary of the English Language*. Boston: Houghton Mifflin, 1981.

Osirin: Ego is concerned with the now. It wants to know who wins and who loses; it wants to know how great the pain and loss might be; it wants to know who walks away wounded in pride and who walks away with the prize; it wants to know whether there will be comfort in making up. That is what egos want to know when they struggle with their partner.

Your soul cares very little about these things. What does your soul ask in the midst of a marital struggle? She sits very quietly, little one, praying. Her prayer is this: "Let the light of God shine through me and through my partner's soul. Let our lights be strong and clear that they may illuminate a corner of those two pained humans. Let us illuminate a speck of those two blind ones that they might see."

The prayer begins again and is repeated over and over, and sometimes it actually works. On rare and wonderful occasions you each turn away from the fray toward your souls. You embrace a light in the midst of blindness and darkness, and the light leads you to safety.

When you fall in love, you think that you have found love. Oh, little one, how rarely do you see that what you have found is merely the ticket of passage. Falling in love as you know it is the beginning of the trip—a trip which can lead to the land of love. But it can just as easily, more easily in many cases, lead to despair and vengeful bitterness.

The ship on which you travel is a most unusual vessel. It is like none you've known in your earlier days, so navigating it is quite a challenge. Many travelers are so ill trained in navigation skills that there is literally little hope as they set sail that they will ever see land again. This sounds very pessimistic, I know. But listen, little one. Listen more slowly. Breathe more deeply and slowly. That's better.

The place where the ship can take you is love. Yet the journey is so unlike what you expect that often you want to give up. People who sign up for a loveboat cruise expect candlelight champagne dinners and moonlight strolls on the deck. If they discover that the plan includes fasting, scrubbing the decks, and setting out in life rafts on turbulent seas, they feel cheated.

The darkness of your night is blindness, little one. You know that ignorance of the law is no excuse. In the same way, *blindness to the light of your soul is no excuse.* You cannot love another without your own light. You cannot navigate the seas of marriage without your own light. Work hard with your partner, knowing that you are working to discover your light. When there are two brightly shining lights side by side, the route toward divine love is as brightly illuminated as if lit by the full moon on a clear and starry night.

～　　～　　～

Osirin: There is not much time today, so I will take over more abruptly than usual. Just let me have the pen.

Becca: Give me a second, Osirin. Let me relax more deeply.

Osirin: That's good, little one. You wish to know more about relationships, so we will talk more today about love between two people. The goal of a relationship is not to find a mate with whom you can live happily ever after. The goal is not to fall in love and stay in love. The goal is not even a satisfying, fulfilling long-term relationship. *The goal is love.*

Both you and Victor struggle a great deal in your marriage. Most of your suffering in these days is for growth, and we in Spirit rejoice for both of you about that. Your labors that are still enmeshed in fear and doubt, however, are distinctly anti-love. Fear can never lead to love. Never. Try to remember that, little one. Fear can never lead to love. If you will remember that as a given, as an unbendable rule of divine law, you will speed your steps toward the love that you seek.

Not all people will or should strive to attain this kind of love. Love is not the only road to travel, little one. Following roads that lead to wisdom, beauty, truth, service, or pure knowledge are equally valid roads to travel. Attempting to find divine love, or at least its earthly equivalent, in human relationships is only one road. It is the road we discuss now because it is your need today.

When you work within a relationship to harvest love, you must remember that you reap what you sow. You know very well that if you wish a garden of summer pinks you sow dianthus seeds, and if you wish an oak tree you sow oak seeds. How often people forget this simple fact in their relationships. People often act as though love should sprout no matter what they sow. Many act as though love is expected to knock on their doors and request admission to their homes.

Love is elusive. Being elusive is not a game it plays with you. Being elusive is its gift to you. It is only through awareness and disciplined effort that you find it. By being elusive, love teaches you to seek it devotedly.

Think again of Mary and Mark. As they journeyed out of darkness to find one another, their error lay in fighting against the wrong adversary. They both fought against the light. Mary fought fearfully by hiding her face; Mark fought warringly by trying to slay the light. Neither recognized that the adversary was their own ignorance of the light. Neither saw that the light they fled was the very thing they sought. Often in your relationships, little one, you cannot see the difference between the light and the dark. You often mistake the light for danger, you become afraid of it, and you attempt to flee it.

People can fear anything on your planet. Absolutely anything. People can learn to fear sunsets, roses, daffodils, and babies' smiles. People can learn to fear anything on the earth, and one of the things most commonly feared is love. This is very difficult for people to hear, because everyone longs for love. Everyone thinks they delight in love. Yet what my eyes perceive is a world full of Marks and Marys.

Your world is not an easy place in which to embrace divine love. There are many obstacles to love between two people, not the least of which are the two egos which are involved whenever two humans join hands in an attempt to love. Egos thrive on fear. Without fear, egos would be out of their jobs! Egos are well versed in the lowly arts of perceiving fear where nothing of danger exists. Once fear has been created, the ego gathers up its armor and weapons in order to fight against it. Just like Mark, the ego draws its sword to ward off the perceived danger, and the sword slices love to tatters. Not that love is harmed, mind you. Love retreats, repairs itself, and returns, but the heart of the swordsman and the heart of his mate do not repair so quickly. Their hearts are left wounded, empty, and pained. How many times have you experienced this, little one? How many times have you turned coldly against Victor as though there were danger nearby?

There is a light—the light of love—shining brightly at all times between you and Victor, but its presence alone does not mean you are *in love*. To be *in love* you must each embrace it and bow before it. Only then will its light enter your hearts filling the emptiness, soothing the pain, and bringing flickers from its flame into the darkest corners of your being.

Becca: I am confused about part of what you are saying about relationships.

Osirin: What is that, little one?

Becca: You say that our error is often fear, especially the fear of love. You imply that if all fear were healed, love would ensue between two people. It's hard to imagine loving with no fear at all. As an extreme example, what about a situation of blatant abuse of one partner by the other? Doesn't it make sense for a wife to fear a husband who beats her?

Osirin: If there is no fear, there is freedom. And if there is freedom, there is movement, growth, and change. Often freedom means moving closer to one's beloved. Sometimes it means good-bye. Sometimes freedom means offering a helping hand to one's beloved. Sometimes it means withdrawing the hand altogether. Freedom cannot lead away from love even if it leads to goodbye, and fear can never lead to love even if it says ''I will stay forever by your side come what may.''

Becca: Thanks. That makes sense.

Osirin: Let me tell you more about marriage. What you know as marriage is not marriage. Divine marriage is a union of two souls dedicated to growing within that union, striving within that union to achieve awareness and love.

Notice that love is the final goal of marriage, not the starting point. Think of marriage as being like a silver urn that holds two souls. Your question is not ''am I in love with this person'' or ''do I love that person.'' Rather, the question is ''do I accept and embrace this urn as a home within which to learn love.''

Your journey with another person toward love is rarely what you hope for and expect. Many people give up along the way, finding the requirements too hard. Often they are. To endure abuse from a mate's unlit darkness is not a path of love. If that unlit and unloving darkness must be rejected, then love is served in rejecting it. To reject love which does not suit your fancy, however, is another matter. You have done that at times, little one. You have sometimes refused to honor love which was not couched in words that you understood or clothed in garb that appealed to your senses.

Divine marriage is a vessel, a living silver urn. It holds two souls within it. It is not a guarantee, a pacifier, an anesthesia, or an escape. It is a vibrating, living vessel—and a possible path to love.

The love that you seek is difficult for me to describe to you, little one. I can only describe it to you from my heart to yours. These words that pour out of your fingers only hint at the meaning of love. I am beaming my love to you now. Feel it.

∼ ∼ ∼

I cannot yet fly through clouds. For a student pilot or a private pilot, darting in and out of cottonballs in the sky is illegal. Only instrument-rated pilots are allowed to do that, and they are allowed that privilege only after lengthy training and extra licensing, only after filing an explicit flight plan for their trip, and only when they are cleared and approved for the flight by the demigods of air traffic control. Zipping in and out of clouds is no simple matter. Why? Because flying through clouds is somewhat like flying blindfolded, and it greatly increases the novice's chances of losing her orientation as to what's up and what's down and plummeting rather abruptly out of the sky and into the earth.

Sometimes human love is a lot like flying blindfolded. I've been studying diligently for several years, hoping that there is such a thing as an instrument rating in human relationships, hoping that someday I'll be able to fly calmly and competently through troubled relationships when I can see absolutely nothing in front of me, beside me, or behind me.

30

One of the most useful navigational tools in my relationship cockpit is the mantra given to me by Osirin that love is the goal. When the going gets rough in my marriage or any other close relationship, I try to pull my airplane out of a spiral of blame, fear, self-pity, or cynicism by reminding myself that this other person, this fellow mortal, does not owe me love; rather, love is the goal we both seek. No matter how the other person feels or behaves, I can reap the rewards of love if only I navigate well—if only I respect both my partner and myself, resist the seductive pulls of self-righteousness and blame, recognize that we are both in route and have not yet arrived at enlightenment or sainthood, and diligently practice the fine arts of communication, patience, and trust. Occasionally I manage all of these cockpit tasks in the proper order, avoiding both spatial disorientation and panic, and soon find myself flying again in clear skies. If I forget the navigational rules, however, I am likely to find myself face to face with the biggest, blackest, meanest thunderstorm east of the Mississippi. No matter whether in the air or in the heart, thunderstorms are no fun.

In relationships love is the goal, not the guarantee. Love is the destination, not the point of departure. Love is the gift, not the obligation. Love is the motion, not the status quo. Love is what is possible to find, not what is probably already lost.

～　～　～

Osirin: As you struggle with relationships, it is difficult to remember that you struggle *with* another person and *against* yourself. Let me say that again. When you struggle in a relationship it is yourself you are fighting against and your partner you are fighting with.

Becca: I think I finally see that, Osirin, but it is certainly difficult to remember when my defenses raise their ugly heads in response to Victor or another person.

Osirin: Little one, remembering that *you are your only problem* is one way to God's heart.

Becca: I like that, Osirin. I'll try to remember.

Osirin: When you struggle for love, you must learn to struggle without ego, for what you call defensiveness and self-protection are, of course, an intricately woven fabric of the ego's creating. Such self-protection appears to be necessary within a relationship. Your ego tells you, "Without my help you would be totally vulnerable here. You could be easily hurt or even destroyed. Let me protect you." In so protecting you, the ego sabotages genuine love each time it approaches.

Remember Mark and Mary. They went out in search of love, but they did so believing in darkness. How could they find light when they believed so deeply in darkness? And how can you find love when you believe so devotedly in protecting your ego?

Becca: I am confused about something, Osirin. Sometimes you tell me that the darkness is bad—like with Mark and Mary. Other times you tell me that I must see it and explore it, and that I cannot love without knowing the darkness.

Osirin: Yes, little one. When I speak in metaphors it is sometimes confusing. There are two types of darkness. The darkness of Mark and Mary is self-protection, blindness, and deafness. It is the darkness of the ego. What you call your dark side or your shadow is different. Your shadow is all that you have hidden from yourself out of fear. It is the treasure chest within you filled with your long forgotten tears, your secret anguish, your abdicated power, and your thwarted dreams. It is the locked away part of your soul. Your shadow is not itself dark; it is hidden in a dark place where you have feared to go. We will talk more about this type of darkness soon.

Becca: Thanks. That helps.

Osirin: All relationships are cut from the same cloth, little one. Mark and Mary don't have to be physically beautiful young lovers in order to make the story true. They could be middle-aged co-workers in a coal mine just the same. Or a mother and child. Or an angry, pained married couple with thirty years of discord behind them. Mark and Mary, and the darkness into which they cast their lot, come in many different disguises.

∿　　∿　　∿

Osirin: Little one, we will talk of something new today.

Becca: Osirin, I am just beginning to grasp the first bit of what you taught me yesterday.

Osirin: Am I going too fast?

Becca: Yes.

Osirin: Don't worry. Write now, absorb later.

Becca: Okay.

Osirin: We need to talk more of trust. What I want you to understand is this: Trust is the deepest feeling you can have.

Becca: What about love?

Osirin: In the truest sense, love is not a feeling. Love is energy. Love is the act of creating or expanding. Much of what you call love with another person is actually trust. I do not mean to create unnecessary complications, but it is important for you to see the difference between trust and love.

Love is the goal, little one. It is the divine outcome of a life well lived, a day well lived, or a relationship well lived. Remember that love is the goal. Trust is the building block. Love is not something you do; trust is something you do. Let me re-explain as this is so alien to your thinking that you will remain confused if I do not speak more clearly.

Becca: Thanks, Osirin. This is somewhat confusing.

Osirin: A bird flies through the open skies. His wings keep him aloft. His wings are love. His flapping of his wings is trust. Is that better?

Becca: Not in the least! But I must admit I'm intrigued.

Osirin: Let me try something a bit different. You lift your airplane off the runway. The airplane is kept aloft by its wings. The wings are love. Your skill at the controls is trust. As you sit in the airplane, you know that you did not design the wings. Even the engineer who did design the wings did not create aerodynamics. Who created lift? Who created birds' wings? Who created air and camber and the magical combination of the two that allows flight?

Think of love, little one. You didn't design it or build it, but you do use it. You create with it. Likewise, you use the wings of the plane to lift you. They allow you to fly. But what good would it do to have an entire fleet of airplanes all with perfectly designed wings if you knew nothing of how to start the engine, taxi, or take off? How much lift would the wings provide then? And what good is it to lie gently in the arms of love if you will not trust? What good is it to open your heart to God if you are not willing to follow? What good is it to ask for love from your fellow man if you do not know how to receive it or what to do with it when you've received it?

Think of trust as the engine, little one. Trust will not get you off the ground. Wings do that. But with no engine you'll never have the opportunity to lift. The engine does not lift the airplane, but it allows the wings to do their work. Trust does not create, but it allows love to enter so that creation may occur.

Becca: I think I see, Osirin. There is a lot about how the airplane flies that I can control. The fact that it flies, however, is not in my control. If the plane crashes it could well be my fault, but the fact that the wing interacts with the air in such a way as to fly is not to my personal credit. The same is true with love. I can't make love be. Love just is. How well I work the controls so that love may enter is what you are calling trust.

Osirin: Yes, little one.

Becca: Osirin, I am very aware that I have no control over your love for me. I did not even know you existed for many of the years that you loved me, taught me, and protected me. Now that I know you, I can receive much more of your love. Trusting you is a very active process. Some days I have to work like mad to ward off my laziness or doubt in order to trust you. I understand what you mean that trust is something I can do. I see, too, that love is not something I do. It is a divine gift, perhaps even a divine given, when I open myself trustingly to you.

Osirin: Yes, little one. I'm glad you see. And the same is true in your relationships with people.

Becca: Show me how.

Osirin: In a sense, love is not to be found with another person, but love can be found within him. Try to see the difference. For example, if love is found with Victor, you become very dependent on his presence. If love is found within him, you are blessed by his presence. If love is found with Victor, then you are passive. If love is found within him, you are an explorer, a seeker, a journeyer. Try to see the difference by yourself, and then try to see it while you are with Victor.

Trusting Victor is the only way you will find the level of love that you seek and that you have struggled to find. Don't turn back, little one. Don't give up. You have trusted before. You know how it feels to remain willing to journey despite pains and obstacles. When you journey with another person, with a partner or a mate, you must be willing to trust.

Becca: Tell me once more, Osirin, what is trust? What does it mean to trust another person?

Osirin: Trust is allowing life to be as it is. Trust is allowing your fellow man to be as he is. Trust means remembering that you are a child of God and that your partner is a child of God. If you truly remember who you are, then your relationships will be filled with active patience and dynamic compassion. *Trust who you are.* Many people ask for love without paying the price of trust. Pay the price, little one. Pay the price gladly.

~ ~ ~

Osirin: Love remains constant. It is only your moods that change. Little one, if you could practice being more like me it would help.

Becca: Osirin, that is the understatement of the century!

Osirin: Listen, little one, and try to feel the way that I love you. I mean that both ways. Feel how much I love you; also feel the way in which I love you. It never changes. The mood which comes and goes is different for you than it is for me. Some days my love for you is expressed lightly, some days loudly, some days with laughter, some days quietly, some days with bouquets of flowers. But the love itself is always, absolutely, unerringly, unendingly the same. In your relationships you often confuse the mood with the love. If love were as fickle as human emotions, you would have a great deal to worry about! You would have a great deal of loss and pain. But love is not fickle.

Becca: Osirin, I am very sad and upset today. Show me what I am doing wrong. How am I missing the point of love?

Osirin: Trust softly, little one, and very lightly. Take yourself lightly! Take love lightly today.

Becca: Am I making it too serious?

Osirin: Far too serious. When the greyness of your mood blocks the reception of love, you struggle hard against love. It is not love that is the problem. It is not Victor who is the problem. Remember very clearly what I have said to you before. No human can bring love to your heart; no human can take love away or bring it back to you if you have set it down along your path. To even the tiniest degree that you see another person as the source of love, you do both him and yourself a grave disservice. Human love is a celebration of two hearts that open and dance, of two souls that recognize the light in themselves and in their beloved. Take the celebration lightly, little one. Laugh and dance and smile. Release the greyness of your mood. Light a candle to the goddess of love within your heart. Sit before the candle and notice that its flicker does not fade no matter how your moods change. Delight, little one. Love never fades, but sadness does.

~   ~   ~

Over many months these meditations and lessons came to me, and I studied them diligently. I was then, and am now, too humble or perhaps too lazy to presume to master Osirin's teachings. Nevertheless, I struggled with the words and ideas he gave me, trying to weave them into my life in a workable, practical way. Words of wisdom on paper, even if they come from my own personal heavenly helper, are still just words. Carefully peeling them off the page and slowing injecting them into my brain is a tedious and often frustrating process. Receiving Osirin's words is not enough. Arguing with him, being lovingly backed into a corner of his design, sparring with him, being brought to my knees by his love or brought to my senses by his wisdom—none of these is enough. His wisdom becomes my wisdom only when I live it. And only then can it bring me peace.

I shared some of Osirin's words with Victor, but most of them I kept to myself. After all, these were lessons I needed and it would have been presumptuous and intrusive to assume Victor was making the same mistakes I was making and needed the same remedial courses I did. You can flunk out of college by making too many F's in physics or by making too many F's in art history. Either way is trouble, but the solution to each of those situations would be quite different. My F's were my own. I learned when to keep my mouth shut, when to keep Osirin's wisdom in my leather notebook, and how to trust Victor's guides to guide Victor. As it turned out, his guides did just fine without my assistance. Our journeys through the pain of separation eventually led to renewal within us both and to a reunion between us.

~ ~ ~

I have never flown into a thunderstorm and, if God and the weather are willing, I never will. I have, however, flown in haze a little too thick and in winds a little too gusty, and I have done a bit of scud-running, flying just below a lowering layer of grey clouds which squeezes the pilot tightly in an increasingly thinner layer of clear sky that lies between heaven and earth.

Journeying into slightly risky realms is a valuable way to learn. A little bit of danger sharpens the senses, jolts the mind into heightened awareness, and stretches the previous limits of one's courage. Loving relationships are guaranteed, it seems, to provide just enough danger to push us past our limits and into our own inner unknowns. Within the arms of intimacy we can be assured that we will be invited to fly through our inner haze, and upon receiving the invitation we have two choices: yes or no.

Intimacy doesn't thrive for long when people refuse the offer to grow, but that is the choice many of us make when we fear the haze and resist our inner darkness. Intimate relationships are schoolrooms. Instead of offering us fairy tale lives of unending romantic bliss, they give us blessed opportunities to learn love. They bring no promises of happy-ever-after, but they do bring invitations for long flights through both sunny skies and thick haze—flights that just might have as their destination the Land of Divine Love.

CHAPTER FOUR

LESSONS ON FEAR

Very shortly after entering my body for this umpteenth incarnational trip I concluded with no reservation that fear is no fun. Throughout my childhood I hated Halloween and abhorred horror movies, never understanding the veiled delight I saw in my older brother's eyes on the few occasions he bribed me into accompanying him to the movies to watch some large beast stomp on skyscrapers in Tokyo. I never understood why the other kids in the neighborhood were thrilled by ghost stories and eery sounds in the night. Even as a child I took fear very seriously and, as energy has a way of attracting its own, fear took me very seriously as well.

As I look back on the monster who destroyed half of Tokyo during his afternoon stroll, I still wonder if the beast is real. Is fear real or is it the residue of a horror movie enacted long ago which holds no relevance in my life today? Is it real or is it an illusion? Can the beast be tamed? Can fear be mastered?

A few decades ago I sat at my desk in a dull and lifeless third-grade classroom, listening as the teacher introduced the subject of long division. After numerous examples on the blackboard, she handed out practice sheets to thirty or so mildly disinterested students. My early education was deadly boring, but long division seemed like an interesting challenge, and I felt confident that I could make friends with these larger-than-usual numbers. Two days later, feeling totally frustrated and defeated, I approached the stern teacher with appropriate trepidation, fought back my tears, and insisted with every ounce of third-grade courage I could muster that it is simply not possible to divide 357 by 21. *Simply not possible.*

On most days I'm still not sure that it is possible to master fear. It is hard to imagine living absolutely fearlessly and embracing life with a stomach that never turns inside out. I hope I will eventually discover that fear, like long division, can be understood, and that in both classrooms there are diplomas for those who persist and for those who endure.

As Osirin guides me through the maze of my fear, I often panic as I round yet another corner and face yet another unknown wall that greets me with no more clarity and no more comfort than the last wall I faced. Each turn in a maze is as alien as the last, no matter how much closer one might be to the innermost resting place. Osirin receives the full force of my trepidation as I resist him, avoid him, and sometimes even sass him with impudence born of anxiety and doubt. Being infinitely patient, he waits longer than I resist. Being infinitely wise, he meets my impertinence with humor, tenderness, authority, or whatever is needed to cool my ire. He allows my fear its existence and its expression, and with the artistry of an angel he helps me transform it into understanding, awareness, and peace.

As I share my lessons on fear, I make no assumption that my fear takes the same form as yours or that the particular flavor of panic that turns my blood cold would do the same to your blood. I also make no assumption that my anecdotes will necessarily provide antidotes to your toxins. I do assume, however, that all of us who inhabit bodies know something of fear and that all of us have asked the question, "What is this beast and can it be tamed?"

~ ~ ~

Becca: How can I push away this fear?

Osirin: Implore me. Ask me to teach you.

Becca: I do, Osirin. I ask until I'm blue in the face.

Osirin: Then your face must be even bluer, little one. You do not turn to me each time you are afraid. You often take a few minutes to tighten your breath, clench your teeth, and increase the acid flow in your belly. All of that turns your face red, not blue. Blue would be a grand improvement at such moments.

Becca: Sorry, Osirin. You're right.

Osirin: Implore me, little one. Implore me with all your heart. You cannot simultaneously implore me and fall victim to fear. It cannot be. I cannot rob from you the pain of being human, but I can help you vaporize your fear.

Becca: Osirin, I am so tired of being afraid. My fear of things dark and evil is exhausting, and on some days my fear of being hurt by other people is crippling. I'm so tired. Please take my fears from me. Please.

Osirin: You stand today in the pit of your fear. Today you face a very hard test as you await a frightening outcome. Believe me, little one, no person has the power to hurt you now.

Becca: I don't understand. Today I feel so vulnerable and small.

Osirin: Oh, my dear little one, you are not so very little. Now listen. Pain does not come from the actions of another person. Pain comes from resisting your own growth. Another person's actions or decisions do not, in fact, affect you. Although we are all one in Spirit and we do touch each other's energy, another person's needs and decisions do not alter the path that you are walking. Sometimes it feels to you that someone else's decisions alter your life in some way. They don't. They don't change a thing. All that you have called losses are merely parts of seeing and accepting the path as it unfolds.

People usually fear change. If your logical mind were to choose every change that occurred in your life, your velocity along your spiritual path would not be impressive! So, you karmically or unconsciously arrange for others to sneak up from behind you on your path and push you forward. That's all it is, but then you label that experience as pain or loss. Label it what it is—a friendly push from behind.

Egos do not take kindly to being surprised, but such is the way of the ego. The fact that your ego does not enjoy or delight in surprise jolts from behind does not negate the gift that is often given to you.

Becca: Why is it so hard?

41

Osirin: Hard? Ah, that is an interesting word. Look up hard and read definitions number 5 and number 7.

Becca: Hard number 5 means stern, austere, callous, cold. Hard number 7 means intense, forceful, keen. Those definitions almost seem like opposites.

Osirin: So, what do you mean by hard? Hard as difficult? Hard as solid? Hard as austerely intense or callously keen? What do you mean by hard?

Becca: Yucky! That's what I mean. I mean hard as in no fun, why me, and give me a break.

Osirin: Oh, that kind of hard. I understand that kind of hard. I call it lonely.

Becca: Lonely?

Osirin: Yes.

Becca: What does lonely feel like to you?

Osirin: Wishing gently, quietly, and tenderly for the reunion.

Becca: What reunion are *you* wishing for?

Osirin: The reunion with you. To be with you in a fuller way than now. And to be with God in a fuller way than now.

Becca: That's very touching. Wishing for the reunion is hard for you?

Osirin: No. To me it is sweet, but it's the same as what you call hard. You see, hard to you is something you wish would go away or end. It is full of fear for you. If there were no fear involved, what would you call it, little one?

Becca: Oh, I see. I would probably call it melancholy.

Osirin: Nice word. Very akin to lonely.

Becca: Yes. Very akin to lonely.

Osirin: So, little one, what does hard mean?

Becca: It means I'm afraid. It means I need your hand to hold and your shoulder to lean on. It means I miss you and I'm homesick for the Light.

~   ~   ~

On a hot, muggy day in July I drove home from the airport angry and exhausted, mercilessly defeated by a few wispy clouds and a lot of haze. For the novice pilot, the first experience of flying alone through the haze of a hot summer afternoon is either an adventure or sheer terror. For me it was terror. Experienced pilots seem to see through haze almost as well as they see on the crispest day in winter when the air is deliciously dry. Not me. I became quickly disoriented, lost all trust in my navigational instruments (assuming that they, too, suffer impaired vision in the haze), and concluded that once again I was hopelessly lost in the sky. Just as I was about to give up and radio for help (properly this time), I glanced down through the haze to notice that the Chapel Hill airport was about half a mile off my left wingtip.

As I drove home in tears I learned again, perhaps for the hundredth time, that the only enemy in the sky truly worthy of my fear is my fear. It's not the haze that makes my blood run cold. It's my own fear.

"Osirin, why?" I called out as I drove home from the airport that day. "Osirin, why am I so afraid again?"

Osirin answered, "Little one, what does *why* mean?"

"No, Osirin. Don't do this to me," I insisted. "Don't make me look up the meaning of the word why. That's not fair. There must be some cosmic rule about this. It's just not fair."

"Why not?" he asked.

"Because I said so," I insisted.

"That's my line," he replied with an almost audible laugh. "Little one," Osirin said in his most comforting voice, "flying is hard. It doesn't matter whether you fly a Cessna 152 or a Boeing 747 or without wings of any kind. Flying is hard. Freedom is hard. No person can learn freedom the easy way. There is no easy way. Fear is not conquered by lying on a soft rug meditating on the radiance of a beautiful crystal. Perhaps love is experienced on the soft rug, but fear is not conquered there. Fear is conquered in life and in living. My words cannot conquer your fear. My words lead you, hold you, teach you, and touch your heart. But my words cannot conquer your fear. To be master of your fear you must fly in all ways, and you must encounter haze and hazing not only in the skies, but in your work, in your marriage, in your friendships, in your activities, and in all parts of your earthly life. That is the way, little one. I love you deeply. Let my love soften you now so that tomorrow you and the haze will have a more equal battle.''

~   ~   ~

Becca: Osirin, I'm in a foul mood today, and I'm angry at you. Really angry.

Osirin: Little one, why are you angry at me?

Becca: Because I'm furious and terrified and you aren't fixing it.

Osirin: Didn't you just today warn one of your clients about expecting God to make every little thing better? Didn't you last week gently instruct your son on the ways of Spirit when he bemoaned that God must not hear his prayers since he has not been granted his wish to fly?

Becca: That's different.

Osirin: And how?

Becca: They were talking about God. I don't expect God to fix everything. I expect you to fix everything.

Osirin: Oh, yes, I see. That's quite a profound difference.

Becca: It certainly is. I would never turn to God when I'm being stupid, unreasonable, and premenstrual. I certainly hope when I die it'll be the week after my period. That's the only time I'm fit for God.

Osirin: And you think you are fit for me today?

Becca: Yes. You're stuck with me. Or so you say.

Osirin: Stuck on you, little one. Not stuck with you.

Becca: What does that mean?

Osirin: It means I love you.

Becca: Stop it, Osirin. I'm furious. Don't soften my heart at a time like this.

Osirin: All right. Rage more, little one.

Becca: I hate this trip. It's too hard. *Just too hard.* When humans are blind they get canes and seeing eye dogs. Blind spiritual seekers seem to get nothing but a hard time. I'd give anything for a seeing soul dog right now.

Osirin: Woof woof.

Becca: Big help you are! I can't see you, I can't reach out my hand to you, and worst of all, sometimes I can't even tell when you're around and when you're not. Osirin, just today I thought I was hearing you when I wasn't. Sometimes I feel that I can't trust you, or I can't trust my ears to know when it's you and when it's not. What if I think I am hearing you and I am really tuning into Genghis Khan or some nasty dead dude like that? How do I know if it is safe to open up to you?

Osirin: You felt the negative energy around you today, didn't you?

Becca: Yes.

Osirin: It scared you.

Becca: Of course it did! What did you expect from me?

Osirin: Little one, what happened when you asked God to free you from it?

Becca: It left me.

Osirin: You felt it leave, didn't you?

Becca: Yes. But for a while I mistook that negative blob of energy for you, Osirin. I don't want to be tricked *ever*.

Osirin: And you will give up on me completely in order never to be confused or tricked?

Becca: Sometimes I feel like it. Sometimes it is very hard to believe in you, Osirin.

Osirin: I understand, little one. Sometimes it is very hard to believe in you, too.

Becca: What? That is ridiculous.

Osirin: Is it?

Becca: I'm right here, visible and all. You're invisible.

Osirin: To you I am.

Becca: I can see this is getting me nowhere.

Osirin: Where is it you want to get?

Becca: I want to get to believing in you fully again. To knowing you're there. To knowing Dad is there. Really there. Not just in my mind, but really there.

Osirin: You want proof?

Becca: A little proof wouldn't hurt, would it? Especially since today I got terrified by some negative blob hanging around my head. Asking for proof on a day like that isn't so bad, is it?

Osirin: Well, what about last night? What about the fact that you knew last night's election returns to the exact percentage of vote before the voters ever cast one ballot?

Becca: Coincidence.

Osirin: How is it, then, that you knew the results of only one race and it was the only race your father deeply cared about? How is it that you clearly heard his voice three days before the election telling you what the results would be?

Becca: Cheap psychic thrills. That's all it is. Predicting election results doesn't get anyone to God. When did you ever read a spiritual treatise that recommended the practice of calling elections three days in advance as a way of achieving enlightenment?

Osirin: Let's see. It seems that perhaps I did read one a few hundred years ago. I'll check my records.

Becca: Okay, your magic is working. I'm calming down. I'm even beginning to smile. I don't like feeling this way, Osirin. I hate feeling frightened and angry, and I despise feeling so out of control.

Osirin: No, little one. You are usually quite graceful in your sadness and pain, and you often welcome out-of-control with open arms. What you loathe is fear, and what you felt hovering around you today was fear. Not a ghost, not a spook, not a Halloween leftover. It was fear, your own fear. I'd recommend that you go get some Kleenex before we go farther. Get the whole box.

Becca: This is a small box. Will that be enough for what you have in mind or should I go out and buy a case?

Osirin: Enough sass, little one. Breathe slowly and deeply. Now I shall tell you more about fear. Your fear is a grey cloud that often encircles your head. It is composed of thoughts that have been given to you by others and thoughts created by you. You must understand the power of your thoughts. Never underestimate the power of your thoughts.

It is a grave error to seek to change external circumstances in order that your fear will disappear. This is very hard for people to understand, and even harder for them to practice once they do understand. Listen carefully, little one: *It is your thoughts that create the external circumstances that appear to frighten*

46

you. It does not happen the other way around. It is with your thoughts that you create that which frightens you.

Let me repeat. Your fear is a grey cloud in your aura. It is a cloud of your creating, and nothing outside of you needs to change in order for it to disappear. What frightened you today was your own fear—nothing more, nothing less. I never trick you; I never have and I never will. It was your own fear that scared you and tricked you, yet it appeared to be caused by something outside of you. Feel your tears arise, little one.

Becca: Why am I so sad? I don't understand.

Osirin: It is not sadness. It is surrender.

Becca: What do you mean?

Osirin: See the child inside of you who has lived in terror. See her, little one. See her clearly. Go to her. Cry, little one. Cry for all the wasted time. Cry for all the sins you have committed out of fear. Cry for all of the people you have hurt out of fear. Cry for all the times you have turned your back on God out of fear. Cry for all the times you have suffered needlessly out of fear.

Becca: I'm sorry.

Osirin: Say it to yourself, little one, not to me and not to the others you have hurt. Say it to you. You have been your own jailer. You have created the fear and then suffered in its cell. Cry, little one. Cry.

Becca: Help me release this fear, Osirin.

Osirin: First you must cry more.

Becca: It's so heavy, Osirin. This fear . . . so heavy. I don't know if I can defeat it.

Osirin: Cry. Yes. Now go lie on the floor and we will begin to melt it. Are you ready to release it to the sun where it can melt like an icicle on a bright morning?

Becca: I think so.

Osirin: Then let's go.

∿　　∿　　∿

Becca: Osirin, I feel great today and I'm ready. Let's go for it! Please show me how to rid myself of fear once and for all.

Osirin: Once and for all? Are you sure?

Becca: Yep, I'm ready.

Osirin: Once and for all as in all eternity or just for now?

Becca: I'd settle for now.

Osirin: Are you absolutely sure?

Becca: Uh-oh. I don't know if I'm sure or not. Is that a risky request?

Osirin: Very risky. Little one, what is the highest you have ever flown?

Becca: Alone? Let's see, 7,500 feet.

Osirin: Were you afraid?

Becca: A little.

Osirin: Why?

Becca: It's more than twice as far to fall as my usual 3,000 feet.

Osirin: Try again. Why were you afraid?

Becca: I'd never been that high before by myself.

Osirin: Ridding yourself of fear would take you much higher, little one. Much higher. Perhaps we should go slowly.

Becca: I'm sure you're right, Osirin. I'll modify the request. Show me what is at the core of my fear.

Osirin: What do you think it is?

Becca: I am afraid of evil.

Osirin: You think that you fear evil, but that's not accurate.

Becca: Oh, yes it is. I still have a very hard time with evil.

Osirin: But you don't fear it.

Becca: Yes I do, Osirin. I do fear evil.

Osirin: Slow down, little one. Slow down.

Becca: Am I missing the point?

Osirin: At those high speeds you nearly always miss the point.

Becca: Is this better?

Osirin: Yes. Now listen slowly. To say that you fear evil is dangerously misleading and misguided. To say that you fear evil turns you into a passive bystander of negativity that seems to impinge upon you. No, you do not fear evil. *Your fear creates evil.*

Becca: Oh, my God. My fear creates the very thing I am afraid of?

Osirin: Your fear creates evil. Relax, little one. We will speak more of fear and evil soon. Rest for now.

∿   ∿   ∿

There have been many times in my life when I have thought of giving up, times when the agony of the struggle was so unbearable that I longed for the finality of defeat. In each and every one of those pits of despair, fear was my quicksand. Sometimes I lay the blame for my pain on life, sometimes I blame my fellow man, and sometimes I blame that amorphous monster called depression. Yet at the bottom of the pit, the villain is always fear. Fear is my karmic Achilles' heel, my spiritual cyanide. With no help at all from the outer world (otherwise known as "reality"), my inner monster of fear can transform light into darkness, peace into panic, love into loathing, and trust into trepidation. What magic my fear can perform. In the twinkle of an eye—poof, misery!

Osirin taught me that my thoughts create my fear. I always believe Osirin, but this pronouncement was so different from everything I had previously believed about fear that its wisdom was hardly instantly apparent. I had lived for many years as though we humans fear things, events, experiences, and situations *outside ourselves*. I had believed that fear is a psychological/biological protective mechanism which warns us of impending danger to our bodies or our psyches. I had believed that fear is "out there" and "real." Osirin did not tell me that this theory is entirely wrong, but his words indicated that it is either mostly wrong or, at the very least, grossly incomplete.

As I looked deeply into my psyche I could begin to see that most of my fears were, indeed, the results of my beliefs and thoughts. There were many beliefs stored in my mind under the heading of "truth" which, as I exposed them to the light of day, held not a grain of truth within them. My thoughts are like a potter's wheel or a painter's brush—they create. My thoughts work on my experiences in the world the way a woodcarver's knife works on a piece of wood. My thoughts literally and pow-

49

erfully create my reality, my circumstances, my emotions, and my fears.

It is no surprise that those thoughts which are heavily laden with fear-inducing energy create fearful experiences. That much I could see. It is obvious to me, for example, that I can convince myself I'm hopelessly lost in the haze when the Chapel Hill airport is directly below me. I can easily create fear in the sky when absolutely nothing is amiss. But some occurrences in the sky, it seemed to me, are genuinely dangerous and deserving of all the fear I can muster. Osirin had taught me several years earlier that there is nothing to be gained in trying to train my body not to be a body. Consequently, an engine failure at 5,000 feet is guaranteed to make my body quiver and to send adrenaline pumping with gusto throughout my bloodstream. No matter how thoroughly I clean up my thoughts, the adrenaline would still pump if the propeller stopped spinning. There is a big difference, however, between an adrenaline rush and fear. The type of fear I am struggling to master is manmade, created by an aberration in my mind, concocted by my own misinformation, mistrust, or misguided thoughts.

One of the primary goals along my path, one which I use as a checkpoint every day, is to learn to greet my fear with patience yet with the firm belief that fear is a distortion of the truth. No matter how loudly my fear screams, it deafens my ears to wisdom; no matter how bright its glare, it blinds me to the light. Fear is a not-so-gentle reminder that there is more to learn, more to see, and more to master.

As usual, it took months of study and practice for these ideas to begin to sink beneath the thickness of my skull into the soft and receptive parts of my brain. Little by little I began to see many ways in which my thoughts create my fear, but I could still not see how my fear creates evil. And I wasn't sure I wanted to know.

One day as I flew I knew there was something wrong with the airplane. When I advanced the throttle for takeoff, the plane rolled through the chilly headwind just as it was supposed to do, but after liftoff I noticed that the RPM's were lower than normal and the climb seemed sluggish. Fortunately I had no tall towers to clear at the end of the runway, no passengers whose weight would slow me down, and no boulders or gold bullion for cargo. I climbed, but very slowly.

The feeling of the slow and sluggish climb was precisely the way I began to experience my meditation. I wanted to know more about how my fear creates evil, yet I didn't want to know. I longed to understand evil more clearly, yet I didn't long to understand. My meditations became a symbol of my ambivalence. I lifted, but the effort was laborious and the rate of ascent was tediously small.

After several weeks of sluggish meditations, my ambivalence gave way to willingness. I knew that if Osirin's choice was to teach me about evil, my only real choice was how long I wished to resist. I finally decided I was ready.

CHAPTER FIVE

LESSONS ON EVIL

When I was a child I sat rigidly in church pews trying to find an interesting fantasy to occupy my beleaguered mind as I tried to tune out the sounds of Southern protestant diatribes on hellfire, damnation, and brimstone. I never knew what brimstone was, but I assumed from the sounds of the preachers' voices and catching the drift of the fiery sermons that brimstone was not a shiny collector's rock to be sought and treasured. I never spent much time contemplating brimstone until Osirin suggested that I look up its meaning. Brimstone, much to my surprise, is sulfur. Plain old sulfur—yellow, sometimes shiny and, in fact, quite collectable.

Maybe if I had been raised a Buddhist, evil would be an easier lesson for me. Maybe if I had been slowly, gently indoctrinated during my childhood to life's occasional pains and agonies, I would have less fear of the types of blindness and suffering that are often labeled as evil. Maybe if I had known that I have within me the source of power with which to face any foe, I would be less intimidated by bad guys. Those were not my experiences in this lifetime, and perhaps they would have provided little or no immunity, even if they had been my realities. I don't like evil. Things that I don't like, I avoid. And things I avoid get sometimes bigger and bigger until they become unavoidable.

When I wrote *Stardust*, I related the lessons on evil that were taught to me by both Osirin and my Guardian Angel. Their words had made me aware that I was being trained as part of my spiritual education to recognize evil and to discover ways to stay out of its clutches. Shortly after *Stardust* was published, however, I felt that my lessons in evil were just beginning. I felt like an utter novice, and knowing very little about something as important as evil concerned me. I began to ask the questions again, ones I had asked a year earlier, "Osirin, what is evil, where does it comes from, and how does it work?"

During the initial weeks of Osirin's lessons to me on evil, I was surprisingly frightened of spooks, goblins, ghosts, ghoulies, and "the devil," regressing to a deeply ingrained childhood philosophy (one that had somehow managed to escape maturation) that professed: There are good guys and bad guys, and if I'm not good enough, God will get very mad and send me off to live forever and ever with the bad guys.

As a child I was taught about a God who, according to some Sunday School teachers, has been known to turn his back coldly on bad children, damning them for all eternity. I assumed that damning souls was something God did when he got very angry. This assumption was, perhaps, a slightly more sophisticated belief than the one that earthquakes and volcanos are caused by feisty, fickle, or furious gods. As a child I didn't worry about angering the volcano gods (as there were no active volcanos near our house), but I did worry now and then about how I could appease the God of the Methodist Church so that he would not damn me to some subterranean furnace.

As the frightened child within me emerged and as I consoled her in her despair, she led me to a startling recognition. The image I had been taught of Satan appeared identical to the image I had constructed of an angry, temperamental, soul-damning God. This awareness was stunning. It brought both horror and relief. If God-in-a-lousy-mood· seemed just like the devil, something was wrong. Something was terribly wrong with my cosmology. What a relief!

I turned eagerly to Osirin, asking him to show me where my errors lay. I was very tired of being burdened by my fear of evil and disgusted with the insidious information I had been taught or had concocted as a child. I was excited to realize that my fear was based on something old, something wrong, and something correctable. I was ready . . . but still more than a little bit afraid.

~   ~   ~

Osirin: I will teach you more today of evil. Do not be so anxious or eager, little one. Relax. You must quest with all your heart and with undying passion, but try to experience undying passion a bit more calmly. Don't rush me. Open your heart more. Put down the pen and open your heart to me.

Becca: I feel nauseous.

Osirin: That's partly the result of coffee on an empty stomach. It is also that lessons on evil are not easy for you. Open more.

Becca: Okay.

Osirin: Remember as you write that this is for you. Yes, we are writing another book, but you cannot focus on that. For now it is you and me, little one. There is no other. No reader. Maybe others will read these very words, maybe not. Just you and me for now.

Becca: I'll remember that.

Osirin: Pause and feel your love for God.

Becca: Yes . . . yes . . . I feel it.

Osirin: Are you frightened of him?

Becca: No.

Osirin: Do you trust him?

Becca: Yes.

Osirin: Do not forget your love and trust of God as we proceed. Now, evil. If you believe that God lives within you, where do you think the "devil" lives? In a dark, dank cave? In a fiery pit? That which is evil, that which falsely pretends to be God is also within you, little one. If you want to face your haunting fear of the devil, go look in the mirror. You'll see him there. Turn gently now to the anxiety and confusion I have aroused within you. You are frightened.

Becca: Yes. Very.

Osirin: Stay near to me. I'll go on. God is not limited to one address. God is everywhere. You know that, but you cannot yet conceive it. The idea that God is everywhere exists in your mind, but it has not yet impregnated your whole being. If God is limited to one address—heaven—then the "devil" must also be limited to one address—hell. According to that view, humans send prayers into the skies to a God who lives many light years away, and the devil lives in hell, sneaking out occasionally to torment humans and to win them over from God. But what happens when God is seen to be everywhere? Then, either there is no evil or evil is also everywhere. And, little one, both answers are true.

Becca: Osirin, am I supposed to be understanding this? Is this supposed to make things clearer?

Osirin: Well, it should be enticing.

Becca: Yes, it is.

Osirin: So, shall we proceed?

Becca: Yes.

Osirin: I feel like writing a poem. Does that suit your fancy?

Becca: Sometimes you are very silly, Osirin.

Osirin: Silliness, as you know, does not end with the physical body, and laughter is one of God's loveliest voices. Now, my poem:

> Evil is a joke,
> A story with an unexpected twist
> Whose punch line
> Punches God.

Becca: Osirin, I'm not sure whether I'd call that silly or *weird*.

Osirin: It's not quite as silly as it appears. Come, little one. Sit over here. Lighten your heart. Smile. You become so somber when we discuss evil. Smile!

Now I'll go on. The surgeon's knife lies on the table. Is it good or evil? Neither, of course. It is the heart and hands of the one who holds the knife that create good or evil. The knife may be used to murder or to heal. The parent's arms reach out to a child. Will the arms hold the child in love or beat the child in fitful rage? Are the arms good or evil? And the *I Ching* or the Tarot cards—are they good or evil? Neither. It is the heart and mind that hold them and ask for their answers that create good and evil.

Do not look for what is good and evil in your world. All is of God. It is the heart and mind that hold a child or a scalpel or the Tarot or a bouquet of daffodils—that is where to look for evil.

When I tell you that evil exists inside you, you become afraid. You react as though I am saying you are overpowered by a negative spirit or a demonic force. It is not so. Give that thought to me. Find it in your mind. Put down your pen and find it.

Becca: It scares me when you say that evil lives inside me.

Osirin: That is because you still don't understand it. Find that fear.

Becca: Here it is. It looks like a disgusting critter, like a cross between a rat and a cockroach.

Osirin: Give it to me.

Becca: Yuck.

Osirin: Thank you. Watch.

(He holds it. It is surrounded by light and then it vaporizes.)

Becca: You're right! You can vaporize my fear.

Osirin: It's a trick I learned an eon or so ago. Nothing to it.

Becca: You are very silly today.

Osirin: Yes. I do so enjoy evil. Ah—see there? Did you see your fear rise again at that moment?

Becca: This is too hard. All you have to do is joke about evil and I begin to freak out. This is awful.

Osirin: No, it isn't. Tedious, but not awful. There's hope for you yet. This is central to all else you are learning, little one, so stay close. Stay with me.

Becca: You are not at all afraid of evil, are you?

Osirin: Should I be?

Becca: Osirin, give me a break!

Osirin: Okay, little one. No, I do not fear evil, for I see it as it is. I am not plagued by false ideas, so I do not fear. I see love, I see light, and I see the twist that can occur, the twist that punches God.

Let me be concrete. That might help a little. You recently had an electrician wire the new well, feeding water into the irrigation system. The wiring was not correct, and when the well was turned on, pipes broke and solenoids blew out of place. Was the electrical power evil?

Becca: No.

Osirin: What was the problem?

Becca: The electrician hooked it up wrong. When the pump was turned on, no solenoids opened. The water was trapped, pressure built up, and boom.

Osirin: Boom is the key. That's what you call evil. Something that is designed to flow doesn't flow. Pressure builds up and *boom*. Boom is evil. Do you see?

Becca: It's a little clearer, but only a very little.

Osirin: One more example. When you take off in your airplane, you pull back on the yoke and the plane lifts off the runway. Right?

Becca: Right.

Osirin: What happens if you lift off at too low an airspeed?

Becca: You might get a sluggish lift or a bounced take off. Or the plane might keep taxiing with a lifted nosewheel until it hits a tree. Or you might get a stall thirty feet in the air. It depends on your airspeed, the length of the runway, and a lot of other factors.

Osirin: The airplane is designed to lift off at a certain airspeed. It's designed that way to lift, fly, and flow. So are you, little one. You are designed to lift, fly, and flow. When you wire your electrical controls wrongly or lift off your runway wrongly, you don't lift or fly or flow. And that is the seed from which evil grows.

Becca: What about external forces like negative energy or negative beings in the air?

Osirin: There are negative energies "in the air," but they have no power over you if you are flowing. If you pray to God or implore me to be by your side, negative energy masses cannot affect you. Little one, study what I have said so far. We'll go farther later.

∾   ∾   ∾

Osirin: If you don't see that evil is of your own creating, you will live your life both fearing it and looking for it outside yourself. It's no different from the search for God, little one. If you look outside yourself, you'll see many of God's gifts and creations. But to know him, look within. The same is true with evil.

Many people presume to know God by only looking outward. Many people presume to know evil only by seeking to avoid it, ignore it, or run from it. The knowledge of God so gained is shallow, and the lack of knowledge of evil so gained is dangerous. Now this next part will not be easy for you, little one. Did you feel your heart skip a beat? Relax. Trust me. Leading you to your own evil is my gift to you, so take my hand.

What you call your dark side or your shadow is your inner repository of unknown and unexplored fear, guilt, shame, doubt, blame, and cold dispassion. It is also the hiding place of unexpressed love, unacknowledged tenderness, and abdicated power. Those ingredients, when mixed together in almost any combination, create evil. Evil is not a being with a forked tail. Evil is something you create day in and day out. Imagine it symbolically as a devil if you wish, for that is not a bad allusion. But you must see that you *create* the devil anew, you conceive him and gestate him and birth him anew, day in and day out. You birth him, he lives, he dies, and the process begins again. So, yes, there are evil energies floating in the air, but they are not living beings. They are mixed-up creations of people that will live only for a while. They are not eternal.

Becca: What about evil disincarnate human souls? What about angry dead people who hang around to haunt others?

Osirin: No soul is evil, little one. The anger and confusion that can result when someone dies is not eternal, so you don't need to fear it. Do you fear an angry six-year-old who throws his food to the floor in a huff? Why should you fear a disincarnate temper tantrum any more than an incarnate one? Help these displaced souls if you can and if you wish, but don't fear them.

Becca: But can't they harm people?

Osirin: Of course they can. An angry six-year-old could possibly hurt you, too, by setting the house afire or throwing his toys at you. You don't live in terror of being killed or driven insane by a six-year-old's tantrums, do you?

Becca: Hardly.

Osirin: The power of an angry disincarnate soul is no different. Move out of its way if you wish, or offer to help if you wish, or enmesh yourself in my love if you wish. Now, let's get back to you, little one. You create your own evil, and that's a lot more to worry about than fearing that an angry disincarnate soul will float through your window at any moment.

Becca: Ouch. I feel punched in the stomach. Stay close, Osirin. I'm scared and I suddenly feel very unworthy of you.

Osirin: I want to show you one particle of evil you created yesterday.

Becca: I guess I'm ready.

Osirin: The way you treated Joanne was evil.

Becca: Show me exactly how.

Osirin: Whenever I use the word evil, translate in your mind this way: "When I am evil, I LIVE backward—away from God." Evil is quite literally LIVE backward.

Becca: Thanks.

Osirin: It will take a while to disinfect the word evil for you. It arouses unhelpful fear and repulsion in you.

Becca: You're not kidding. This is grueling.

Osirin: The way you treated Joanne was evil because you fell into fear. You feared being out of control, being overwhelmed by difficulties, and being washed away in a high tide of enormous problems. You blamed her behavior for your fear. You acted as though she created your fear. You acted coldly and without love, and that was evil. You acted out of fear, and that is the fabric of which you create the black shrouds of your own living hell. Enough for now. We must go slowly here. Rest for now. Rest in the arms of my eternal love for you.

~ ~ ~

My hunger to understand more about evil and darkness was almost insatiable. Each time Osirin spoke of evil, I was both frightened and intrigued. The awareness that evil is my creation, not a dangerous "him" or a scary "them," gradually became a comfort rather than an ominous scarlet *E* I felt cursed to wear. If there is a literal devil, and if one of his assistants trails me like a secret agent conniving every way imaginable to design my undoing, the best I can hope for in this life is that I might have sufficient energy and intelligence to avoid becoming his victim.

If, on the other hand, evil is of my own making and the symbolic devil is my own bastard child, the best I can hope for in this life is freedom, joy, and the enduring awareness of God.

~   ~   ~

Osirin: There is something I want to explain clearly. In your attempt to understand evil, try to see the difference between beings and energies. Beings and energies are not the same. You, little one, are a being. What you use to create with is energy. Think of energy as similar to the ingredients for your dinner. You use the ingredients to create dinner. Each ingredient has an energy of its own. Carrot energy is different from lettuce energy is different from pasta energy. You combine them to create dinner.

You are working in your everyday life with many different energies. There is the energy of joy, the energy of courage, the energy of giving, the energy of power, the energies of pain, fear, despair, happiness, peace, and many others. You combine them to create the life you live and the world you see around you. One person may like a lot of avocado energy in his salad, and another may like a lot of peace energy in his life. Few people claim to like a lot of fear energy in their lives, but many earthly chefs use it as the primary ingredient in their daily living. Some favor hate, others dismay, others garnish generously with despair.

There are energies in the earthly plane in great quantity which are non-existent or which exist in only small quantities on other planes. Some of the energies that we have in abundance on our plane you have in very short supply on your plane. Energies such as peace which abound here are ones you struggle diligently to achieve.

The energies with which you create your experiences and your reality are, by divine plan, quite diverse. In your life you have a great deal of choice. There are many, many ways in which the energies or ingredients of life can be blended and mixed, and there is an infinite array of outcomes. Those creations which are based heavily on joy have a much higher probability of being tasty and nourishing than do those whose main ingredient is fear.

Concoctions made essentially of hate are much harder to digest than those made of acceptance. There are some energies and some combinations of energies that produce creations so indigestible, so malodorous, and so toxic to spiritual well-being that they deserve the title of evil.

Think of a chemistry lab. If chemicals are mixed in a certain way and fire is added, an explosion can occur. Imagine that the chemicals are ones that, when ignited, emit toxic fumes. People would be wise to stay clear of those fumes until they dissipate, but there is no sense in ascribing to the fumes a personality. The fumes are not out to get you or to turn you away from God. The fumes are merely toxic and will kill you if you breathe them. They are detrimental to your well-being, to your health, and to your ability to remain in physical form. Once the fumes dissipate, however, they are gone. You can imagine that they evaporate or disappear; you can imagine that they become so diffuse as to be unrecognizable and harmless. Whatever you imagine, the truth is that they are no longer potent. Their energy is gone. This is the way of evil. When it is no longer empowered by man, it is gone. It does not live in a dark hole waiting to attack. It is gone—until it is again concocted and empowered by man.

The ancient wise ones knew this. They created rules of living which led unaware people away from those chemicals on the shelf which might explode in their faces. What has been lost over time is the underlying truth. There is no behavior that is necessarily evil. It is the energy within the behavior that creates either evil or loving joy.

Becca: You say that nothing is inherently evil. I almost understand that, but how would murdering an innocent child, for example, ever be considered not evil?

Osirin: Some chemicals on the shelf are much more dangerous than others. Only a very tiny pinch of the murdering-small-children chemical could cause a very dangerous explosion. That chemical could possibly be mixed with enough compassion, love, tenderness, awareness, and peace that it would not produce evil. It is possible, but I would not recommend that anyone try it! Stop for a moment, little one, and reflect. Do you understand what I am saying?

Becca: Yes, I think so. This is making more sense to me than ever before, and I'm not resisting your words as you speak. Thank you, Osirin. Thank you.

Osirin: You have resisted this lesson mightily in the past!

Becca: Why is it so hard for me?

Osirin: For two reasons. First because you fear. Evil is a very easy thing to fear. Secondly, as a child your religion taught that evil is to be avoided, not understood or mastered. That which is avoided gains great power, as you know. I have explained evil to you in many different ways. Remember that my explanations are all allusions.* I cannot show you evil or let you hold it in your hands. It is not physical. It is not spiritual. It is astral. Do you know what I mean by that?

Becca: I think so. You mean that evil lives not in the physical plane—in other words, not because of physical form. Also, evil does not live in your plane. It exists between the two, sort of, or in the astral plane. Evil is like the meat in a bologna sandwich. Right?

Osirin: As allusions go, yes, that's right. I have deep compassion for your hatred and fear of evil. I wish you could see it as I do, for then you would smile instead of fear.

Becca: Smile?

Osirin: Oh, yes, little one. Smile. The way you smile when your son says he hates you for making him go to school. The way you smile when weeds pop up in your garden. The way you smile when your car runs out of gas or the winds are gusting too much for you to fly. Those things are annoying, but beneath the annoyance is a slight smile of awareness—knowledge that each is your own gentle fault, an unwelcomed Godly gift, a disguised blessing, or a lesson to be learned.

Evil is not abiding. In fact, everything which is astral in nature is in constant flux. The astral itself is enduring, but that which moves within it is not. Evil comes and goes and changes form often, whereas the light of God is utterly and absolutely forever.

Becca: Is that why people came to believe that there is a devil who changes form frequently in order to trick people?

*Please see page 93 for Osirin's and Guardian Angel's explanations of allusions.

Osirin: In a way that is so, but the answer is more complicated than that. People began to ascribe these characteristics to their concept of the devil because they were unaware of the ways in which they themselves select from the available energies, mix them, and create with them. The human mind has great power to create. Yet it also has great power to deceive itself. When it creates something which causes itself fear or pain, or when it perceives fear and pain in the creations of another, it will often deny responsibility for these creations and label them the work of an evil outsider. The belief that Satan is changeable and seductive is a projection of the mind. It is the human mind itself that is very changeable and seductive.

Becca: Why are our minds designed in this way? It seems like a lousy design.

Osirin: Ah, little one, that is a very hard question. Will you forgive me if I answer in an evasive way?

Becca: Sure. Answer any way you'd like.

Osirin: Human existence and life in human form
   Is a test of one's mettle
   To face against impossible odds
   The reality of God
   Who lives within the muck and mire
   Who lives within the love and fire
   Within, without, and beyond.

Becca: Nice poem.

Osirin: Thanks.

Becca: So the reason that our minds are designed that way is "just because." Right?

Osirin: For now. Or you might say the reason is "just because I said so."

Becca: I'll buy that.

Osirin: Good. I'm offering a discount today on evasive answers.

Becca: I love you deeply, Osirin.

Osirin: I know, little one. I know.

~   ~   ~

Becca: I have a very specific question for you, Osirin.

Osirin: What is that?

Becca: Are you saying that there is no devil?

Osirin: Oh, little one, how you do long for concrete answers! No matter how I answer your question, you can misinterpret what I say.

Becca: You know my heart and mind so well, Osirin. Speak to me in any way you will. I'll listen and I'll work hard to hear you clearly.

Osirin: My dear little one, *God is real*. That lesson is my gift to you and you need no other gift. Beyond that, I join hands with you in your struggle to understand as you and I dance together and play together, soaring through the cosmos explaining this and explaining that. God is real, little one. That is the vessel on which we fly. All other explanations are merely clouds we soar above and through and beyond.

Becca: I understand.

Osirin: Then I shall answer your question. God is real; the devil is an allusion. There is energy in your world that is anti-God, but the fact that energy can go against God does not necessarily mean that there is an embodiment of that power any more than the fact that airplanes sometimes crash means there is a large, literal hand in the sky that pushes machines out of its territory. Energy that goes against God is powerful, and mankind has grown to fear it. All energy in concentrated essence is very powerful.

People in your culture usually personalize only the power of love, calling it God, and the power of anti-love, calling it the devil. But God is not only the power of love; he is much more than that. *God is.* In your culture you no longer personalize the power of the sun, the moon, the rain, the stars, the wolf, the bear, or the hundreds of God's other faces. The world is not either/or, good/bad, God/Satan. It is so much richer than that! God is real, little one. Return to where we began—God is real.

~   ~   ~

65

Becca: All these lessons about darkness, evil, and fear are a lot to learn, Osirin. You're teaching much faster than I can absorb this stuff.

Osirin: I'm a bit ahead of you?

Becca: A bit.

Osirin: Let me teach you. Little one, slow down. You may not know it, but your energy is jagged today. I can't get through your jagged aura very easily. It feels like flying through turbulent air. Don't jostle me so much. Settle down!

Becca: Is this better?

Osirin: Yes. Now let's continue our discussion of evil. I want you to remember that *evil means to live backward and away from God.*

Becca: I remember.

Osirin: The ingredients of evil are any things that reside in what you call your dark side or your shadow. Your inner darkness is not evil. The darkness is that within you which is unfaced, unmastered, unknown, or feared. It is that which is shut away. It is that which is truly part of you but which you do not avow. You must always remember that your inner darkness is not evil. It is your commitment to remaining blind to your darkness that creates evil. For example, little one, your inner power is part of your Godness, yet often your power resides in darkness. Your power has lived in darkness much of your life. Remember, Guardian Angel told you long ago that half-hearted power is dangerous. He could as well have said it is evil. When your power "sneaks" out of its dungeon, it expresses itself as sarcasm, fury, bitterness, or rage. When your power is full, whole, and well lit by the God-light within you, it is expressed in some form of love.

Other people hide away their gentleness, and half-hearted gentleness hurts just as much as does half-hearted power. Others lock away their fear, not acknowledging its presence or its fierceness. To cage a tiger in darkness is no solution. Enter the cage. Know the tiger and set him free.

Evil lives only as long as you feed it with the food of your soul. Don't feed it and it dies. I do not say it leaves you alone; I say *it dies.* It is possible to live in a world free from evil. It is possible, if all men come to know themselves as children of God and fear and loathe nothing of the Godness within them.

~ ~ ~

Each time I fall into my old habit of thinking that evil is a big bad dude wearing a red suit whose one delight is ensnaring unsuspecting souls and seducing them into an eternity of fiery damnation, I feel sick. That idea holds no light for me. It does not send me running toward God for protection or toward Jesus for salvation. In fact, it makes me crouch like a frightened animal in a dark corner of life, distrusting both God and Jesus, and wishing for a ticket out of this ungodly mess called Earth.

On the morning after my Dad died I learned that life is an eternal treasure and that the Earth is both precious and Godly. I realized soon thereafter that my quest was to follow the Light— whatever Light I could find—and trust it to lead me home.

A pilot can make her way from the East Coast to San Francisco by VOR-hopping—traveling from one navigational fix to another to another and so on across the continent. VOR transmitting stations are dotted throughout the country, and all a pilot needs to do is tune one in and follow. That's what I do in the sky. It's what I do along my spiritual path as well. I tune in whatever Light I can find, and I follow it until it leads me to the next Light.

I have made a few serious navigational errors on my spiritual path just as I have in the sky. I have occasionally followed the right signal in the wrong way, only to discover that I've managed to get myself lost again. Other times I have followed the wrong signal in the correct way, and that creates an even more confusing dilemma for both pilots and spiritual seekers. When that happens, a pilot has no choice but to stop in her tracks (as best as she can while traveling 110 knots), throw out the old plan, quickly devise a new plan, ask for help from the nearest radar facility, and resume careful, cautious navigation.

Following the wrong VOR happens to most pilots at some time in their flying career, and following the wrong allusion happens to most seekers sooner or later. Fortunately, when one allusion doesn't lead us toward the Light, we can tune in another one, just like tuning in a different VOR.

Each of us must choose, day in and day out, what allusion we will follow and which VOR we will use to guide us home. On my journey, the Satan VOR is not helpful in navigation. Every time I tune it in, I get lost. So I have quit using it, at least for now. Maybe next year it will make sense as an enlightening allusion, maybe not. For now I keep a sticker on my instrument panel that reads: SATAN VOR—temporarily or permanently out of service; do not use for navigation; it won't lead you home.

As soon as I accepted that no matter what the Church says, no matter what the neighbors say, no matter what some of my family and friends believe, and no matter what the modern translation of the Bible is interpreted to say, that I don't believe in the devil, I began to relax. I finally accepted that tuning in the Satan VOR makes for a rough and dangerous ride, one which takes me very far away from home. Once I accepted what is true for me, I found I could learn about evil in other ways. I found I could learn about evil with an open mind, not one shut tight with terror. I found I could join God's army to fight, not against an unconquerable foe, but against my own blindness and the darkness within my heart.

On most days now, I am not afraid of evil. I see it as a perversion of life, as living backward. Evil is like a grotesque piece of pornographic "art," a sad distortion of Godness that can perhaps be resculpted, redesigned, and returned to its rightful spot in the world.

Evil is no longer a horrifying, unconquerable, overwhelming, sadistic force that lives outside of me. It is now a normal part of life—the backward part, the part that leads away from home. There is nothing insolvable or eternally damnable about being lost, waylaid, ignorant, blind, bitter or self-righteous. These are errors and backward ways of living just as following the wrong VOR is a backward way of flying. All pilots do it, just as all journeyers stop along their path every now and then, concoct a bit of bad brew, serve it up to their friends, and wonder why everyone gets sick. It happens to all of us, not because some guy in a red suit loathes mankind or holds a serious grudge against God, but because navigating home is hard work, and because very few on this earth are master navigators who never err.

CHAPTER SIX

DIVING TO THE SKY,
SOARING TO THE SEA

Often throughout this book I have compared the experience of being on the spiritual path with entering a university. Actually, that's a questionable analogy. When you enter a university you are given a handbook which tells you exactly how many courses you must take to graduate, how many hours of your life those courses will devour, whether or not you have to suffer through physics or pre-Aristotelian philosophy, and exactly when you can expect your sheepskin. You know what you have to do, when you have to do it, and how well you have to do it in order to graduate. At regular and pre-determined intervals along the way you are given a grade point average that announces with no uncertainty whether you are a scholar or a flunky. With each course you are given a syllabus which outlines the lectures and books that will guarantee your success. Universities are logical, ordered, predictable, and systematic. Not so the spiritual path.

On the spiritual path, courses appear in seemingly haphazard order and tests often occur with no warning. On Monday the unannounced mid-semester exam is on material you've never read on evil. You read the material on Monday night only to be presented on Tuesday with lessons on peace and tenderness. Wednesday brings fear and terror, and on Thursday there is a pop quiz on the philosophical bases and practical implications of the karmic interaction between delight and despair. Friday's test covers material presented three years earlier on obscure elements of reincarnation and past life fiascos.

The weekend—ah, the restful weekend—that's when you get to integrate all the seemingly unconnected, unrelated lessons of the week. Saturdays are puzzling, but finally sometime late Sunday afternoon there's a glimmer of understanding that perhaps it was Wednesday's fear that created Monday's evil, which is not contradictory since time is not linear anyway. And probably the tenderness of Tuesday was a pre-cognition of what Wednesday needed. Most likely, you discover, Thursday's despair paved the way to the past life remembrances of Friday which were based on the evils of Monday. Yes, yes, now it all makes sense! Finally on Sunday afternoon it's all so clear. The professors smile, then class begins again on Monday.

∿   ∿   ∿

I was at the beach on vacation with Victor and our seven-year-old son, Josh, looking forward to having plenty of time to fly. I scheduled a lesson with an instructor, asking that he give me a check flight in order to approve me as qualified to rent an airplane from the local flying school. I also asked him to teach me what I needed to know about beach flying. After an island tour and one cross-country flight, the instructor turned me loose saying I needed to fly alone. He gently refused to fly with me any more, and to my total surprise he encouraged me to plan a long solo cross-country flight.

To a student pilot, the long cross-country flight is the pinnacle of novice-hood. It is a solo flight of at least 300 nautical miles which includes landing at three different airports. In a Cessna 152, when the wind blows gustily against your nose you fly only slightly faster than the cars on the highways beneath you. At that pace, 300 nautical miles alone in the sky is no small potatoes.

I was more than surprised at the instructor's suggestion; in fact, I was stunned. "Are you sure?" I asked. "The long one? Are you serious? Me?" A small voice inside me wanted to yell, *"I'm entirely too little and too scared to fly 300 miles!"* I realized that would be an unsophisticated thing for a student pilot to scream in the middle of an airport, not to mention unnerving to the dozen or so passengers awaiting the next commuter flight. I kept my jaw clenched and my mouth shut.

On the way home I picked up a newspaper and a cup of coffee then secluded myself on the deck of the beach house to think about the instructor's outrageous proposal. Two delighted gulls flew in tandem overhead and the newspaper headline read: "19-Year-Old Pilot Flies Single-Engine Cessna From Helsinki to Red Square; Lands in Downtown Moscow; Big Soviet Shake-up." Maybe the headline wasn't that long, but it seemed to go on forever. That kid was 19 years old and landed, an hour or so after his touchdown in Red Square, in a Soviet jail. If he had the guts to fly to Moscow, I could surely fly to Myrtle Beach.

I called my instructor and said, "I'll do it." I began the plotting, listing, drawing, planning, and studying that has to be done for a flight. How many miles is this leg? That leg? In what direction? With what winds? How much fuel do I need? What's the air temperature? What's the time required? What altitude should I fly? What's the radio frequency for this airport? That airport? How much fuel? Who do I call if I'm lost? What do I do if I can't reach him? What if my radio goes out? What if all my electricals go out? What if my engine quits? What if . . . what if . . . what if . . .

I woke up the next morning, pulled the curtains, and saw the first dark skies of the week. Part of me was sad and part of me was enormously relieved. Although I had said I would do it, most of my psyche preferred to be lazy, stay at home, lie on the beach in the rain, and say into the grey clouds, "What do you expect? No novice in her right mind would fly today. It's not my fault."

As I walked beneath the grey clouds later that day I heard Osirin say gently, "You're not ready."

"Not ready for what?" I asked.

"Not ready for the cross-country," he answered.

"What do you mean not ready?" I asked indignantly. It's one thing to know deep in your heart that you're not ready. It's entirely another matter to have someone else tell you you're not ready, even if that someone is the most dearly beloved of all gurus and the most trusted of all teachers.

"What do you mean not ready?" I repeated. "I have studied as much as I can study and I've done every bit of pre-flight planning that can be done. Several instructors have told me I'm ready. What's the problem?"

"You're not ready, little one," Osirin said.

There are many times when I hang on Osirin's every word. At other times, however, I ignore him. Spirit guides are usually not terribly intrusive or insistent. They honor the principle of free will and leave us alone to fall on our noses all by ourselves when we insist on the right to deafness. I switched my hearing aid to "off" and left it there for the rest of the day.

The next morning when I awoke, I looked out the window to see a clear sky. "Super," I said, "this is the day."

I went downstairs, called the flight service station to get the weather forecast for my route, and heard an encouraging report. As I was re-calculating some of the last minute flight figures, I said to Osirin, "It looks like this is the day. Am I ready?"

Osirin replied, "Little one, you are not ready."

"Not ready? Give me a break! Look, Osirin, I don't know whether this voice I am hearing is you or the voice of my fear and doubt. This is very confusing. I don't know what this is about, but I know I have done all the planning I can do. If you don't want me to fly, then show me. Please show me. Change the weather or do anything you choose. If you don't want me to fly, you'll have to show me."

"Little one," Osirin said with a gentle grin in his voice, "changing the weather over the entire East Coast is something of a trick."

"I'm sure you can manage it," I teased. "You must have connections. If it's too tough to change the weather, do something else. You can mess with any little wire in that airplane that you want. Foul up the fuel gauges, zap the radios, or scramble the VOR. I'll get the point and I won't go. But you need to show me. Otherwise, I'll assume this is my fear talking and I'll fly as planned."

After I had driven two miles toward the airport, the skies became dark. Very low clouds moved in and parked themselves directly overhead.

"Osirin, you really didn't have to go to all this trouble just for me," I said with a silly grin, expecting the clouds to lift at any moment.

"You are not ready," was Osirin's only reply.

I hung around the airport for an hour or so talking pilot talk with all the pros who wondered along with me when the skies would clear. They didn't clear, so I went home to wait for better weather. At 2:00 I called the airport to cancel the plane so another pilot more gutsy than I might fly around the island during the afternoon. At the same time I made reservations for a 3:30 flight on the shiny red biplane I had seen flying up and down the beach giving rides to tourists. If I couldn't fly the cross-country that day, I decided to soften my sorrow by taking Josh for an open-cockpit biplane ride. A few minutes after I made the call, the skies cleared and the day became as glorious as any beach day should be.

On the drive to the airport Josh confessed his ambivalence about the biplane ride. In an attempt to teach Josh the courage I never possessed as a child, we had a long and impassioned talk about guts and fear. I assured Josh that many things in life which seem to be frightening are really exhilarating if only we will give them a chance. I explained to him that fear has often stopped me and courage has often freed me. As we parked at the airport, Josh was ready for the flight. The kid was psyched!

We walked onto the field and Josh climbed up on the wing of the shiny red biplane. The pilot gently coaxed him as Josh peeked into the open cockpit and examined all the instruments. I was encouraged to see Josh's leg swing over into the passenger's seat, but then it froze. A few moments later his little leg slowly withdrew and he turned around. Tears rolled down his cheeks as he said, "Mommy, I don't want to. Please, Mommy."

I reached for Josh's outstretched hand then turned to the pilot and said, "I don't want to push him or scare him. You and I have both done our best to encourage him, but this must not be the day. I'm sorry to mess up your schedule, but this isn't going to work."

"Let Josh stay here with my wife," he said, "and you come fly with me."

"Thanks a lot," I replied, "but I don't want to pay so much money to sightsee around the island. I sightsee every time I fly."

"We aren't going to sightsee," he calmly said.

Many things in life which seem to be frightening are really exhilarating if only we will give them a chance. I said it to my son, but do I believe it? I quickly jumped into the cockpit, strapped myself in like I've never been strapped before, and said to the pilot, "Hurry up. Let's go before I chicken out."

The pilot was behind me, but I felt very alone in the front seat of that tiny red airplane with no roof. The air was broken by a wing a few feet over my head, but otherwise it was me and the sky. I waved to Josh from the open cockpit as we lifted into the air. The pilot flew the plane a short distance from the beach and said, "Are you ready?"

"Yes," I replied stoically into my mike. I reminded myself that I am not afraid of death. Falling is a little scary, I admitted as the airplane climbed steeply, but death is really okay.

As the pilot talked to me through the earphones, we soared higher and higher, aimed straight for the sun, suddenly banked sharply to the right, spun toward the sea, then rolled over and over again toward the land. Again we soared upward, spun, rolled, dipped, and looped. "How are you doing?" the pilot asked.

In response to his question I heard someone laugh. It was as though the laugh came from a hundred feet leeward, yet the voice sounded familiar. In a second or so I realized that the laugh was mine. From that moment on my only response was laughter. I loved it! My eyes saw earth then sea then sky—then sky then sea then earth—then the other way around—then again and again. We dove to the sky and soared to the sea. We spun around the earth and the earth spun around us. And I laughed and laughed and laughed.

~ ~ ~

The next day I woke up to the clearest skies I have ever seen. The weather experts at the flight service station couldn't find a single cloud within hundreds of miles, and the wind was calm.

Once again I calculated the last minute data for the flight and once again I began my drive to the airport. Sometimes I forget to ask Osirin the questions that need to be asked, but he never forgets me. On the way to the airport he said gently, "Now you are ready, little one."

"I am?" I exclaimed with surprise, almost as though there had been no yesterday and no time when I hadn't been ready.

"Yes," he said.

"Osirin, thank you, thank you. Why am I ready today when I wasn't ready yesterday? I didn't do any extra studying or any more detailed planning. What is the difference?"

"Little one," Osirin said, "yesterday you laughed when you could have been afraid. Yesterday you found joy in the presence of fear. Yesterday you let yourself delight in the face of what you could have experienced as terror. Now you are ready. Fly, little one. Fly!"

The 300-nautical-mile flight that followed this blessing was relatively uneventful. All pilots have stories to tell, and any pilot can make a story out of any flight. I have stories I could tell of that trip, but they are are short and sweet. I made a few mistakes, but they were small ones. Fear did not fly with me that day. I had faced fear the day before and I had laughed.

~ ~ ~

Spirit leads us by the hand if we offer our hands. Sometimes we know the path we walk. Usually we don't. Sometimes we are lead into the skies toward a known destination. Usually we only think we know where we are going.

When I dove to the sky and soared to the sea, I laughed. I didn't have time to wonder where I was going. Up, down, left, and right happened so quickly that there was little separation. Sea and earth and sky rolled into one. And, thank God, someone else controlled the airplane. My job was only to laugh.

In my laughter I was liberated from one more layer of fear. Like an onion being slowly peeled away, my fear exposed one more of its faces to the light of the summer sun and dissolved into delight.

CHAPTER SEVEN

LESSONS ON POWER

When I entered the University of Power and Freedom on my thirty-seventh birthday, I knew slightly less than nothing about power. I was raised in a culture that valued meekness in its girls and sweetness in its women. It just wasn't proper (pronounced prah-pah) or nice (pronounced with three syllables) for a Southern belle to burn her hoop skirt in the streets or defile the statue of Scarlett O'Hara that stood in the town square. In the pocket of the South where I grew up, sweetness was a virtue of such elevated status that it outranked even honesty, integrity, or courage as a pathway to heaven. In that neck of the woods, sweetness was far more venerable than power. It is no wonder that I entered adulthood with many misconceptions about power and very little motivation to seek it.

As I began to study power, my misconceptions became quickly apparent. I had assumed that power would make me tough, would free me to be a bully when it served my needs, would raise my level of assertiveness with push-in-liners at the grocery store, and would make me freer to yell at sour store clerks or surly IRS agents. I soon learned, however, that Osirin was not interested in assertiveness training. Power and yelling at store clerks appear to have very little in common.

In my dictionary, power has fourteen definitions only one of which so much as hints at God. According to definition number 13, power is the sixth group of angels in the hierarchical order of nine. Included among definitions 1 through 12 is the mathematical definition of power, as in "ten to the third power is 1,000;" there's the optical definition, as in "wow, that's a powerful telescope;'' there's the electrical definition as in ''the power just went out;'' there's the physics definition which I never understood in physics class and still don't understand in the dictionary; and there are a bunch of definitions having to do with various aspects of being a bully or pushing somebody around. None of those definitions provided me with much clarity, so I asked Osirin, ''What is power? What is this kind of power you are trying to teach me? Osirin, often I'm unable to tell whether I'm being powerful or simply bitchy. Am I walking today in power or in quicksand? I want to learn more about power.''

Osirin: Little one, begin by remembering what Guardian Angel taught you several years ago about power.

Becca: I wrote in *Stardust* his lesson to me about power. I have reread *Stardust* many times. His words about power have always been fascinating to me, but I have never fully understood them.

Osirin: Perhaps he was a bit premature in giving you those words, but seeds properly planted germinate in their proper time. Now you are ready to read his words again. Go get *Stardust* and read those pages.

Becca: Here it is. He said: ''Power is not force, yet power does have force within it. Power is not control, yet power often results in what appears to be control. Power is a life force, just like the lightning. Lightning occurs quickly. So does the thunder that follows in its wake. The traces that it leaves in the atmosphere are purifying. Sometimes it destroys something as it releases its power, yet that is the way of life. Destruction is not bad or evil, but the chaos of half-hearted lightning—that is bad. The destruction caused by such blockages, the blockages of half-hearted lightning, is far more potent than the potential danger of standing under the tallest tree in the field during an intense electrical storm.''

Osirin: Read on.

Becca: A little later he said, ''That fear of power in the pit of your stomach—that is the main block between yourself and your soul.'' Osirin, he seems to be telling me that living with half my power is potentially more dangerous and more destructive than living with no power at all.

Osirin: Yes, little one. He also says that the fear of your own power is the main block between your "self" and your soul. Do you know what that means?

Becca: I am beginning to see. I see isolated instances, but I can't see the whole picture. Just today when someone was angry at me and I stood firm, when I breathed deeply into my belly and responded with compassion, I felt powerful. At times like that I understand what power is. It is not control, assertiveness, or aggressiveness. It feels like a peaceful strength in the pit of my stomach. When I feel that type of power and wholeness, I feel that I am living soul-fully.

Osirin: Yes, little one. Power is peaceful strength. Power is like a graceful column holding up the temple of your soul. Power is quite literally the same as your life force. Do not think of power as being control over someone or something. In fact, you may change the word "power" altogether if you wish. That word is much abused in your culture. Power is life force. Power is movement. Power is the freedom to move, grow, and live.

When you live without power, you live in great pain. Your body is immobilized. You can barely breathe, and you feel as though life is being crushed out of you. And it is. When you have no power, you have no life. I certainly do not mean physical life; I mean *Life*. Plenty of us in Spirit have more Life than lots of you in bodies.

Becca: I've certainly noticed! Osirin, did I become afraid of power because the women in my culture did not teach me?

Osirin: Your family, your culture, and your world have not fully supported your power. However, you must realize that this world is not a place where power is given. Power is given when life is breathed into you by God. The world is a schoolroom in which you struggle to possess that which is rightfully yours. In a sense no family can teach power. Families can only encourage children not to drown in a sea of fear, guilt, or doubt.

Let me tell you a story. In the days when people believed in goddesses, the goddesses were seen as possessing enormous power. They held the keys to fertility, to victory in war, to the healing of pain, and to the abundance of the crops in the fields. They were seen as possessing power *over*, but they were rarely seen

81

as givers of power *within*. They were worshipped and asked to use their power benevolently, but they were not seen as gentle mothers who would share their power with their children. Times have changed. You on earth are beginning to learn of the goddesses within yourselves. You are beginning to learn that power lives not only within the realm of some faraway gods and goddesses. Power is life, and that is what you are. It is within you. Power is the possession of the goddess, and you are the goddess.

Becca: Osirin, that is so very beautiful. Thank you.

~ ~ ~

Becca: Osirin, I still don't understand my fear of power. I know that I was not taught as a child to be powerful. I was taught to be nice, obedient, and kind, but not powerful. Just because I was not taught it, why would I necessarily fear it?

Osirin: Because you are human. Fear of power is simple. Fear of power is the fear of paying the price of being fully alive.

Power is given by God. The fear of power is taught by man and by the physical realm within which man is born. Be compassionate toward those who taught you this fear. You are passing on the fear to your son, Josh, no differently than it was passed on to you. You wish your son comfort and safety. Do you not call behind him as you ride bicycles together warning him to slow down and to be careful? You do not want him to pay the price of being fully alive, for sometimes that price is pain or even death. In your love for him you teach him to be less than fully alive. This is the way of the world, and you are not faulted for it. Josh must learn to integrate safety with freedom, judgment with spontaneity, and compassion with independence. He will struggle the same as you are struggling now, and he must overcome some fears which, little one, you are teaching him this very day. Be gentle with yourself, as this is the way of the world.

This is a great paradox of human life: to be loved, to be loving, and to be powerful often seem to be in conflict. It appears that you cannot have all, that you cannot be all. It appears that you cannot be loving, powerful, loved, and free in this world, especially not all at the same time and all of the time.

Becca: Bingo, Osirin. That's most definitely how it looks.
Osirin: Smile, little one. It's possible. It's a delightful riddle.
Smile with me. Do you see what a delightful riddle this is?
Becca: Sometimes, my friend. Sometimes I actually do.
Osirin: I wish you could see how delightful your smile can
be. Smiling at the riddle puts a shine in your eyes. Smile more.
Frown less.

~ ~ ~

Becca: I feel horrible today, Osirin. I'm pessimistic, sour,
irritable, and depressed. Can't you do anything to help?
Osirin: I love you, little one. I have told you that a thousand
times. You have known it a thousand times, but today it doesn't
help.
Becca: What am I doing to block the love and help you are
giving me?
Osirin: You are holding too tightly to your interpretation of
what the problem is. Tell me what you think the problem is.
Becca: For starters, I've been reading through my journal,
remembering many difficult and painful experiences of the last
year and a half. That has made me very blue. Also, I am thoroughly exasperated with myself as a pilot. I feel about as com-
petent in the sky as a turkey buzzard would feel in scuba gear.
I don't think I ever want to fly again.
Osirin: Neither of those is your answer.
Becca: I didn't think they were, but that exhausts my list of
likely candidates.
Osirin: Then shall I give you the answer?
Becca: An answer from you, my dear friend, would be most
appreciated.
Osirin: These are times of trial.
Becca: You say that often, but I have never figured out what
it means.
Osirin: Look up trial, definitions number 2 and number 4.
Becca: Trial number 2 is the act or process of testing, trying,
or putting to the proof by actual or simulated use and experience
as in "a trial of one's faith." Yep, that one fits. Let's see, trial

number 4: a state of pain or anguish caused by a difficult situation or condition as in "the fiery trial through which we pass." Gee, thanks a lot, Osirin. Two very upbeat definitions.

Osirin: You enjoyed that?

Becca: Immensely.

Osirin: You asked to learn power, didn't you?

Becca: I'm not sure I asked, but I naively said I was ready.

Osirin: That's about the same as asking.

Becca: Okay. So I asked.

Osirin: Power is not an easy lesson.

Becca: Osirin, you're making me feel very sassy. None of the lessons you give me is easy. Do you call trust easy? Do you call fear easy? Do you think the lesson on abandonment was a picnic? What's the deal telling me power isn't easy?

Osirin: That's better, little one. Do you feel a little less depressed?

Becca: Clever trick. Yes, I do feel less depressed. Now I feel angry. By the way, you haven't given me an answer.

Osirin: Are you sure that I haven't? Look within.

Becca: You must have been a Buddhist monk in your last life. You often teach me in ways that seem like riddles or tricks. Were you Buddhist?

Osirin: Look within.

Becca: Within what, Osirin? Within me or within this crystal I'm holding?

Osirin: They are one and the same.

Becca: When I look at this crystal in just the right way, I see a very brilliant light.

Osirin: Look at that light. Move the crystal slightly and you no longer see it. Move it back and the light is there. Your eyes may not always perceive it, but the brilliance is there. In one sense the brilliance lives deep within the crystal, and in another sense it is reflected by the crystal. Its brilliance is so great at times that it is too much for your earthly eyes. You have a crystal like this within you. It is your power, your life force.

Becca: Osirin, I am feeling peaceful and very nearly happy. What did you do to me?

Osirin: I flipped your circuit breaker, little one. Every now and then your fuses pop and you feel as though you have no radiance within you. Remember the crystal within you. Remember the light.

I am not your power. I love you, but I am not your power. You are the channel of your power. You are life and you are power.

~   ~   ~

Becca: You say you are teaching me power. Osirin, what is power?

Osirin: Do you remember that I answered that question last week?

Becca: You did?

Osirin: Yes. Truth is not like clothing fashions; it does not change with the season. I could give you the same answer in different images, different colors, or different words. At the risk of being redundant, I will tell it to you in precisely the way I did last week. Power is life and life is power.

Becca: Now I realize why I forgot. I didn't get it then, and I don't get it now. What will I be able to do with power that I can't do now? Will I be able to uproot large trees with my bare hands? Osirin, I'm sorry to be so dumb. Can you explain it to me any more simply?

Osirin: What is the opposite of love, little one?

Becca: Fear, I think.

Osirin: What is the opposite of freedom?

Becca: Fear, I think.

Osirin: What is the opposite of power?

Becca: Oh, my goodness . . . fear, I think.

Osirin: And what is one of your lessons every time you soar three or four thousand feet above the earth?

Becca: Fear.

Osirin: When you are frightened at 3,000 feet, what do you fear?

Becca: Falling out of the sky.

Osirin: Are you sure?

85

Becca: No.
Osirin: What is the worst thing that could happen?
Becca: Crash-and-burn.
Osirin: Try again.
Becca: Oh, I see. The worst thing would be staying on the ground and living my life in fear. The worst thing would be refusing to live fully or fly freely just because sometimes I'm afraid.
Osirin: That's the worst. What would you lose?
Becca: Freedom. Power. Courage. Maybe even love.
Osirin: Now you tell me. What is power?
Becca: Freedom.
Osirin: And what is freedom?
Becca: Power.
Osirin: And what is love?
Becca: Freedom from fear and the power of being fully alive.
Osirin: Not bad, little one.
Becca: Thanks, Osirin. By the way, what about those big trees? Will I be able to uproot them?
Osirin: That depends.
Becca: Depends on what?
Osirin: On whether you learn to drive a bulldozer.

∾   ∾   ∾

There was a time when I believed that power was the stuff of which bullies are made and that freedom meant never having to say you're guilty, much less wrong or sorry. Now I know better. I still don't know a lot, but I do know better. Power is the juice that flows when I am living fully and wholly. Sipping the juice of power doesn't make macho men or liberated women; it makes real live men and real live women.

I had been a student in the university for over two years before I was allowed to register for Power & Freedom 308: *Power and What it Feels Like in Everyday Earthly Existence*. The course lasted for three days, and class met for 24 hours each day. For 72 hours I lived in a strange new land, and during that time I soaked into my core the awareness that I am power and power is me.

As usual, pain had led me to the door of this particular classroom, and without the nudges that pain provided, I might not have pleaded for a course ticket. It is not pain that teaches me, but pain certainly has a way of knocking me to the ground and, when I find myself on my knees in the mud, I usually decide that learning my lesson is preferable to wallowing in the mucky quicksand of self-pity and despair. In this particular case, I prayed as deeply and as genuinely as I had ever prayed, asking for a glimpse of the truth and for a key with which to unlock the mystery of my blindness. Other people "push" me into pain and "cause" me agony, but they do not hold the keys to the truth. My fellow humans, those other fallible earthlings whose errors bring me pain, are both professors and fellow students in the divine university.

On the night when my fellow earthling knocked me down, I couldn't sleep. As I tossed and turned, I prayed to God to show me the truth that lay beyond my pain. In my half-sleep I saw a temple from which light radiated in a rainbow of beautiful colors. I intuitively knew that I could not live permanently in the temple as long as I remain in physical form, but a ray of light broke off from the rainbow and formed an umbilical cord between me and the temple of my dream world. Jesus stood beside me and said, "This is the temple of the light of Spirit."

Suddenly I knew. In a state of half-awake sleepiness, in that mystical land that lies between waking and sleeping, I knew that the temple is real. *Literally real.*

In my sleeplessness that night the temple became far more real to me than my physical body. I knew that when I die, my body will crumble, but the temple will never crumble. I could also see that the harsh words and actions of the person who had hurt me that day were not real. No human ego is real; no defensiveness is real. The pain that they cause, when exposed to the temple's rainbow light, is washed clean. In the middle of that night, reality was re-defined for me almost as dramatically as it had been on the morning after my father died. I knew with every part of me that my real self is Spirit, my real home is the temple, and my real feelings are power and freedom.

For the following three days every part of my self was home, and every part of my self was bathed in the rainbow light. In those three days I learned that power is much quieter than I had expected. When there is nothing to say, nothing needs to be said. When there is nothing to give, nothing needs to be given. "Nothing" is a gift, and when given from power, it is a vibrant and energetic gift.

Power is much gentler than I expected and much more humble than I expected. It contains no judgment of self or others, and it spends remarkably little time in evaluation of any sort. Power is much more direct than I expected; it says what is so and lives what is so. Power has a deeper voice than I had known before, a gentler touch, a stiller sleep, a freer physical movement, a clearer insight, a lighter walk, a fuller wail, and a louder cry. Power knows herself to be whole. She is all of me. She is Life.

Power is also more tiring than I expected. After three days I reluctantly knew that I needed to return to the world of the ordinary and the mundane. The total aliveness of power was more than I could yet sustain, so I asked the goddess of power to retreat for a while.

"Please understand," I said to her. "I love you deeply, but I cannot yet live like you each and every day. You are too big for me, or I am too small for you. I hope to be ready soon. For today, however, I am Becca. Not a divine Becca, just an ordinary Becca. Help me make this ordinary Becca big enough to fill a corner of your shadow. For now, love me while I'm less than you."

The goddess retreated as I asked, and I settled back into the routine of everyday life, everyday personality, and everyday ego. But reality has remained new and different. I did not return to the same world I had left. The rainbow light is as close as I allow it to be, and the temple is forever real.

~　　~　　~

As I approached my fortieth birthday, I was tempted to search my numerology books for the special meanings of both four and zero, but I resisted that urge and turned my attention deeply inward instead. I retreated to the Temple of the light of Spirit and asked myself, "What more do I know of power and freedom today than I knew three years ago?"

At first no answers came and yet, instead of feeling despair about my ignorance, I sat quietly and waited. "Surely," I comforted myself, "these three years of adventure on the land and in the air have taught me something. Wait."

Gradually I began to see isolated bits of truth like various pieces of a jigsaw puzzzle that did not yet fit together into a recognizable picture. I wished that my lessons during these three years had led me to a complete and infallible understanding of power and freedom, but they hadn't. So I gathered up the puzzle pieces that I found around me, cherishing each as a precious gift from my soul and from my Spirit teachers and trusting that if I guard these pieces carefully enough, someday I will discover more. And someday, somewhere within this divine universe, my soul will take those pieces I've gathered, join them with other pieces she has collected over the centuries, and fit them together to form a splendid picture.

As I reviewed the preceding three years, I began to understand what Osirin had meant when he said that the preposition belonging with freedom is not "from," it's "within." There is nothing to be free from; there is a lot to be free within. My battles against fear, particularly the fear of evil, had led me to a deep awareness that there is nothing to run from. Fear has become a signal for me to sit very still and to go deeply inside myself for both comfort and guidance. Fear is at the same time the greatest block to freedom and the clearest messenger that freedom is possible if only I will learn the lesson that is mine to learn.

Freedom is aliveness—full responsiveness to all the life within me and around me uncontaminated by fear in any of its guises. Power is also aliveness. Power is allowing all of me, every nook and every cranny of my being, to emerge from hiding, to be bathed in God's healing light, and to be held in the arms of my soul. Power is living life with all my heart, not just the pretty parts or the easy parts, but all my heart.

Power and freedom are not two different qualities, but then neither are love and truth. Neither are peace and joy. There is only one God. His many faces shine inside me no differently than they do in my garden or in a sunset. I struggle to find power within me in order to better know God within me. When I discover a bit of my power, beside it smiles freedom which holds hands with both compassion and courage. On the right of courage stands trust, to the left stands peace. There is only one God, and touching any one of his faces inside of me brings light to all of me and brings me one step closer to home.

CHAPTER EIGHT

GRADUATION

I recently found in my mental mailbox a large parchment scroll, rolled neatly and wrapped in white paper stamped with this return address: University of Power and Freedom, Physical Plane, Earth. That's all. No zip code. Just Earth.

I eagerly tore away the paper and unwrapped the scroll hoping that perhaps this was my diploma of graduation. I had been enrolled in the university for nearly three years, so maybe, just maybe, I had graduated without knowing it, missing the graduation ceremony while I was off in the sky playing in an airplane. Perhaps the Board of Governors was presenting me my certficate of achievement in absentia.

I don't know why I'm always so eager along my spiritual path to graduate. Graduation is never an ending, rarely a dramatic change, and sometimes it's not even a relief. According to definition number 2 in my dictionary, to graduate is to change gradually or by degrees. According to Osirin, graduation is "a gentle movement from here to there; an inching of your heart and mind, hand in hand, toward your soul; a smile in the direction of God; a request for your next adventure." Graduation doesn't fix anything that isn't already fixed and it doesn't exempt the recipient from further study. The parchment scroll wasn't a diploma. It was a letter from Osirin and read:

There is no freedom in all the universe greater than the freedom you possess today. There is no power in all the universe mightier than the power you possess today.

Study if you wish. Struggle if you must. Journey farther if it pleases you.

But remember, little one, remember. Work to remember. Ask God that you might remember. Hold my hand and let me help you remember. It's all within you, little one. The freedom you seek is your aliveness.

You don't have to have a body in order to be alive, but since you do have a body, you have no choice but to be either alive within it or dead within it.

It's so simple. The key to both freedom and power is so simple: Don't be dead. Let yourself know with clear honesty what it is that deadens you. Look sternly into the eyes of fear, bitterness, laziness, apathy, and false longing.

Be alive. Be fully alive. If you follow this simple mandate, freedom and power are as inevitable as sunshine, rain, and wind.

At each and every moment that you are fully alive, your power and your freedom shine as brightly as the North Star. Is that really so hard to believe?

> *Bless you, little one,*
> *Osirin*

P.S. Guess what? You graduated many, many years ago. Congratulations. Now your job is to remember.

CHAPTER NINE

WORDS OF WISDOM

___

GUARDIAN ANGEL on ALLUSIONS

"There is one reality—that is God. In the universe as you know it there are no other realities. All else in your eyes, in your understanding, is allusion," Guardian Angel said.

Osirin had spoken to me earlier about allusions. I felt compelled, however, to look up the word again, this time in my new dictionary. An allusion is an indirect, but pointed or meaningful reference. An allusion is different from an illusion in that an illusion is taken to be reality; it is an erroneous perception of reality. Illusion implies being deceived by perception or belief. Allusion, on the other hand, refers. It *refers* to something other than what is seen.

"Remember," Guardian Angel continued, "only God is real. *All else is allusion.* Absolutely all else.

"Good allusions point to God. Bad allusions do not necessarily point away from God, but they muddy already unclear waters, they cloud already hazy eyes, and they confuse already ignorant minds.

"Your search . . . is not for truth since you already know TRUTH: God is the One and Only One Truth. There is no truth to search for. What you search for is the purest of allusions, the most accurate of pointers to God, the clearest of teachings . . .

"What points you toward God is sacred for you. Abandon God for no one. Abandon your allusions for no one, or you risk the despair that darkens the soul's light. Alter your allusions only when clearer, brighter ones enter your heart as teachers of Truth."(Reprinted from *Stardust*, pp. 95-97)

OSIRIN on ALLUSIONS

Never look directly at the sun. In an eclipse, look only at the miracle through deflectors. Your eyes can burn if you look directly at the source of power. Enjoy allusions, and know that they are the sweet children of Truth. (Reprinted from *Stardust*, p. 69)

OSIRIN on POWER AND FREEDOM

Little one, my love for you is eternal. I wish you could feel that, for its truth would comfort you deeply in these days of trial. Your friend the eagle soars with both power and freedom. Your friend the bear trods the earth with both power and freedom. It is not one or the other. The lessons are not separate. They are the same. Powerfreedom could be one word, little one.

What are you struggling to be free from? Nothing. *What are you striving to be free to?* That is the more useful question. Working hard to become free from anything or anyone is utterly futile, little one. See clearly. To be free *from* is to escape. There is nothing and no one you need to escape. Sometimes you think of freedom as an end to your pain and fear. Not so. It is the other way around. Saying goodbye to fear and unnecessary pain brings freedom on its wings.

OSIRIN on ONENESS

When you look deeply into the eyes of another, you touch yourself in his eyes. You touch your true self, not your ego or your romanticized ideal. There are many people on the earth within whose eyes you have seen your self, could have seen your self, or will later see your self. That you see yourself in the eyes of another is not magic or special—it is merely the essence of that which is true and real.

Oneness with another person can never be painful. You experience pain only when human definitions and human needs are superimposed over spiritual reality. That is when your pain is born.

OSIRIN on PAINFUL LOVE

In my world love has no pain. The cause for pain in your world is the work of the ego. Its roots, as always, are fear and doubt. Love is an intense experience, and the more intense the earthly experience, the more intense the doubt can be.

To understand the hurts of human love, you need to see more clearly the difference between pain and sorrow. We in Spirit feel sorrow; we do not feel pain. Pain is not an element of spiritual relationship, but sorrow is. Sorrow is like sadness for what is not. Sorrow is sadness for the daffodils that did not bloom or the fruit tree whose fruit was blighted before it ripened. There is always another time, another year, another season. Sorrow is the expression of sadness for what is not in this time and in this season, and sorrow in this season keeps the doors open for growth to occur next season.

When love is not possible today, open your heart to sorrow but say goodbye to pain.

OSIRIN on CHANNELING

Becca: Osirin, I have read a number of channeled books. Very often I am amazed at how similar your words are to the words of other guides. Sometimes, however, your words are different, and your style is certainly different! You rarely speak to me about the mechanisms of human consciousness or how the universe works, though other channels often write of those things. Can you explain that to me?

Osirin: First remember that channeling simply means listening clearly to that which has always been near. Everyone channels. You are a channel, little one. Think of it as being like a TV channel. Channel 5 is a CBS channel, channel 10 is an NBC channel, and channel 12 is the Disney channel. Each channel picks up certain waves in the air. No channel picks up all of them. Each channel is unique, yet the same show may appear on two different channels.

Human channels are the same. I speak to you about your experiences and I teach you through your experiences, so what you channel will be filtered through your mind, your experiences, and your personality. I do not talk much about how the cosmos works because that is not your interest or your need at this time. I talk to you about you, little one. Remember, you are not channel 5 or channel 12. You are channel Becca.

OSIRIN on ASKING FOR PROOF

Don't look for proof, little one. Look for love. Love lasts a lot longer than proof. Proof lasts only as long as your intellect cooperates, which is an infinitesimally short period of time under the best of circumstances. Love, my dear little one, is a bit more durable.

OSIRIN on KARMA AND GUILT

Guilt does not exist in my realm. Guilt is an aberration. Consider the law of karma. All acts have consequences. That is not meant to frighten you. All thoughts have consequences, too. Everything that you do, think, say, or feel has a consequence. All energies within you are creative powers, and they all create. You are usually not aware of their creativity, but that does not change their ability to create. You must begin with an understanding of this principle.

Negative thoughts create negative energy patterns. Sometimes they materialize, sometimes they don't. Regardless, they create a form which acts within your experience of the world. You create it, but you often feel as though you were its victim. Remember, you created it.

When you fully recognize that you create, guilt is not possible. You create that which you need in order to learn. Whether you learn from what you create is entirely another matter. I am not saying that everything you create is fine and lovely. It is not! But everything you create is for a reason. If you hold within you the knowledge and faith that it is created for a reason, then guilt is irrelevant. What becomes relevant is how well you master the lessons you created. You write your own lesson plan, and it is up to you to master the lesson. Guilt is an escape. Guilt simply says, "I feel badly that I created this lesson for myself and now I will indulge in self-pity instead of learning my lesson."

Do you wish a higher choice than guilt? Then be totally awake, alive, and responsible. Study your life with all its failures. Study with an open heart. Study with tender compassion toward yourself. In that classroom, guilt will find no home.

OSIRIN on HIS FEELINGS AND EMOTIONS

Osirin: I am glad to be talking and writing again. My writing hand, laying idle for a while, began to itch. A cosmic itch, figuratively speaking of course. I enjoy writing with you.

Becca: What is enjoyment like to you?
Osirin: Like the smile you smiled early this morning when you saw the sun rise from the airplane window. Or like the love you felt last night as you heard your friend's prayer. Or like the peace and reassurance you feel at this moment as you write my words. It's like that.
Becca: Osirin, do you have emotions?
Osirin: Yes, little one, but my emotions are not like yours. Yours are volatile; mine are not. Mine are chosen by me, not imposed upon me by some inner or outer generator of feeling. My emotions are part of my energy. I use them and choose them when they enrich my experience. Perhaps you could practice the same. When there's nothing to feel, no emotion needs to be emoted. Try a little silence, little one.
Becca: I love you so very much, Osirin.
Osirin: I know, little one. That's enough for now. I'll be close to you today. Love me, but do it quietly. Try a little less emotion today. Just love me very quietly. Very quietly.

A LOVE LETTER from OSIRIN to BECCA

The fingers that type these words are mine. They can speed through time without any help from you, but your help is quite appreciated. It is hard to communicate to you when your ears are sealed and your heart is sealed, but today you fly in my energy and on my wings. Today we soar. Be my wings on earth and let me be your wings in the sky.

OSIRIN on PEACE

Osirin: There is something I want you to know about peace, but words cannot say it. Watch for it, little one. Watch quietly and clearly.

(I closed my eyes as Eastern Airlines flight 231, on which I was an ordinary paid passenger, flew above the clouds. Several minutes later I opened my eyes and looked out the window.)

Osirin: How would it be to live here? Just like this?

Becca: It looks beautiful.

Osirin: And what about living here?

Becca: As scenery goes, it's gorgeous, but what do souls do here?

Osirin: Oh, the usual. Live. Love. Create. Are you concerned that you would be bored here?

Becca: Yep. You caught me again, Osirin. It's beautiful, but it's just air and clouds.

Osirin: No movie theaters?

Becca: I'm not that tacky, Osirin.

Osirin: No gardens?

Becca: Yes, I am that tacky.

Osirin: Look into the clouds. Do you see the gardens?

Becca: Oh, God! Yes! I do.

Osirin: Describe them.

Becca: Well, they are . . . they are white . . . and sort of rolling . . . and deep. Words don't do it. I can't describe them.

Osirin: Close your eyes again. Now open them. Do you see the life force dancing through the sky?

Becca: Yes, I think so. I think I can almost see it.

Osirin: Watch the life force as it dances. Now listen, little one.

> Peace comes in seeing what is. Peace does not
>   come in transcending what is.
> Peace comes in embracing life. Peace does not
>   come in mastering life.
> Peace comes in loving yourself. Peace does not
>   come in knowing yourself.
> Peace comes in living your fullest. Peace does not
>   come in trying your hardest.
> Straighten your seat back, little one. This airplane
>   is going to land.
> My love to you and peace to your heart.

99

OSIRIN on KARMA

You do not understand why your grief and sorrow are so deep today. It is because you are cleansing a piece of your karma, little one. Don't ask more questions about that now. Just accept it. No good would come from details, so trust me. What good would be done if today I told you that you were once a rapist or a murderer or a thief? You do not always have to be told your illness in order for it to be healed.

This is a special day, little one. The day when karma lightens is a day of celebration. I know you can't perceive it as clearly as I, but it is cause for great joy in my realm. Think of us celebrating for you even though your work is still hard and your road is still long. We often celebrate for you at times that you have no awareness at all of our celebration.

OSIRIN on JOY

Enjoy the joy that you feel today. This joy is your birthright. Welcome it. Embrace it. It is truly yours more than you know. It is not a reward for doing well or even a reward for correcting your errors. It is simply your birthright and a gift from your Father who loves you.

OSIRIN on UNCONDITIONAL LOVE

Unconditional love is unconditional—not only based on what the other person does, but based on what you do as well. See clearly, little one, that unconditional love has no conditions, none, on you or on the other person. It must always be that way—total and complete. You often forget half the formula; you often forget that unconditional love coming from you must be unconditional toward you as well.

100

GUARDIAN ANGEL on DEATH

Death is the entrance into the known from the unknown. All that lies beyond death is known, and upon entrance into it, the fear of the unknown vanishes.

Death is the entrance into the known. What man fears as unknown is not unknown at all. What you live day to day in the physical plane is unknown. The physical plane is unknown in that its meaning is not completely penetrable. Meaning is available to man in the physical plane only to the extent that he is willing to know death.

Mystics often speak of light bodies or light beings. You now have a physical body within which is housed your light body. Your light body is not exactly hidden, but it is obscured by that which surrounds it. The physical body is not right or wrong in itself, it is simply a densifying force. It creates density around light.

Death approaches each man as a kind and loving teacher. Death is always a kind and loving teacher. If light is to shine through a stone, the stone may not be comfortable. If light is to penetrate into the bowels of a cave that has been dark for a thousand years, the cave may not be immediately grateful. Death does not usually seem like a kind and loving teacher for it defies the physical. It is also the ultimate offense to the ego and personality. Death totally annihilates the ego with the softness and caress of its light.

Man recycles over and over through what he is not, and it is all designed to lead him to what he is. It is all designed to lead him to God. Death is the gentle teacher who takes him by the hand and leads him to himself—to God.

To help someone prepare for death, you must help them see who they really are. Prepare them to experience the joy and majesty of who they really are. Prepare them for the journey into truth. Prepare them for awareness that they are magnificent beings. This is a great shock to most people when they die. Expecting this surprise helps prepare them for the full majesty of the journey.

Death teaches you who you really are. Working with the dying teaches you who you really are. Remember, however, that if you are to teach someone that he or she is a magnificent being, you must first recognize that you yourself are one.

OSIRIN on HUMAN PROBLEMS

Each of your problems and struggles is a tool, little one. Each problem is like a paintbrush or a small pot of colored ink. Each is a tool with which to draw another detail on this grand canvas called Becca's Life, so treat each one as such.

When you feel fear arise inside you about these problems, honor it. Welcome it. Say to it, "Ah, dear old friend, welcome! Come in. Sit with me. You are the trusted guide who always shows me the limits of my wisdom and the outer edge of my understanding. Show me what opportunity you bring me today."

Do not recoil from your fearfulness or your powerlessness. Embrace them, little one, for they will lead you to the very part of the inner jungle that remains dark and unexplored.

OSIRIN on PREPARING THE GROUND

These are times of quiet, little one. Quietness is not deadness. Often when you are quiet and slow, you fear you are losing ground. This is not so. You are tilling the ground. In tilled ground there is nothing majestic to behold, but a majestic garden must begin with well tilled soil. Listen now. Listen to the hum of the tiller inside you.

OSIRIN on PEACE AND CREATIVITY

Let's talk today more about peace. You often think of peace as a state of feeling good. Remember what I said recently about your moods—they are very fickle. Feeling good is a mood; peace is not. In physical terms, peace does feel good, but when the good feeling disappears, peace does not. It is possible to be deeply peaceful in the midst of intense trauma or during times of very unsettling and upsetting emotions. Peace is not tied to your emotions.

You have felt deep peace a few times in your life, especially in your dream world. In those moments you experienced something akin to joy, but you felt a deep silence rather than excitement. Within peace there is a sense of knowing and power, as though all that enters your being is within your understanding and within your power to either embrace, create, or change. There is a flow within this space quite different from anything you experience in physical reality. Everything is much more fluid than you know it on your plane. Change is easy. Movement is almost effortless. Growth and creation are the building blocks of all experience. There is absolutely no fear. New experiences bring with them a sense not unlike what you call curiosity, yet there is no excitement. There is curiosity, vitality, and alertness. All of these states are enduring ones. What you call excitement is a human mood; it is fickle and changeable. In the process of creation within the realm of peace, vitality is enduring.

OSIRIN on HUMAN LOVE

Becca: Osirin, I can't figure out this problem, and it hurts so much. I don't understand human love. If this is human love, what's the point? If I open my heart and this happens, why bother? Who needs this? However, if I say no to human love, the lights go out. Osirin, I'm totally stuck. I don't get it.

Osirin: Little one, go slowly. Easy. Stay with me. Complain more and stay with me.

Becca: I'm too tired, Osirin. This is a horrible week. Too much is happening, and I can't process all this data at once. I'm sinking and I'm too tired to fight.

Osirin: I know, little one. Complain even more.

103

Becca: You've taught me that human love at its best is a remembrance of divine love. I don't expect anybody in a body to be God. At least I don't think I expect that much. But what good is a remembrance of the divine on Monday which feels like a stab in the back on Tuesday?

Osirin: It feels like a stab, little one. It feels like . . .

Becca: You mean it isn't a stab, but only feels like one?

Osirin: Human love is a tool and a vehicle. It is not your answer or your reward. It is your vehicle to ride to God's door. You see it too often as your reward. You see it as your goal. You see it as your possession. None of those ideas is helpful. You must see human love as your vehicle. Sometimes your car runs out of gas. Does that mean your car is a failure? Do you give up on cars? Do you give up on transportation?

The soul of each human is divine, yet no human is your vehicle. Nobody can ride you to God's door. The interaction and love between you and another person, however, is a blessed school, and learning the lessons within that school can speed you on your way to God's door.

Respect your brothers and sisters. Honor them as divine beings. The interaction between the two of you is the vehicle. Do not mistake the interaction with the person. Your friend, your son, your husband, your partner, your colleague—each is a divine being hiding behind a sometimes hurtful ego. Find the tenderness behind the hurt, find the forgiveness behind the pain, find the peace behind the disappointment.

Human love is never perfect, little one. Divine Love is never less than perfect. Rest gently in those two assurances.

OSIRIN on HEAVENLY HUMOR

Becca: Are all spirits as silly as you are?

Osirin: Not all. But heaven is, indeed, a happy place. It is not only the angelic choirs, the crisp white wings, and the cute cherubs that make heaven happy. We tell lots of heavenly jokes to bide our time.

Becca: To bide your time until what?

Osirin: To bide our time until all humanity can smile with us, laugh with us, love with us, and live with us. We are biding our time until all you earthly beings can truly understand our smiles and truly share in our joy.

CHAPTER TEN

OSIRIN'S POEMS

A NEW DAY

There is a new day dawning.
  Perhaps you've noticed; perhaps you haven't.
  Draw no conclusions based on whether or not you've
    noticed.
The sun, of course, does not rise.
  Neither does it set.
  The beautiful skies occur as you yourself move, not as the
    sun moves.
  You stand on the beach marveling at the beauty and change
    of the sun.
Face it—you're the one moving and changing.
  Not the sun. You.
Tomorrow morning as you watch the sky come alive, think of
    yourself rising.
  You are the change.
    You are the movement.
      You are even the colors.
Give credit where credit is due.

TOYS

All the toys with which you play
  And all the troubles with which you fight
Are merely exercises
  And reflections of that which is real.
Enjoy your toys
  And your troubles
And keep looking upward.

FLOWERS

The flower opens slowly
Each petal following its own path
Questioning not its outcome or destiny.
  Just opening.
Hope in your heart that the petals of flowers never develop
  intellects.

THERE IS NO RUSH

There is no rush. Don't hurry yourself.
You have infinity to work out your salvation.
If you wait until tomorrow, it's only one more day of pain.
  And next year—it's only 365 days more of blindness.
  There's no rush.
And if you wait until you have all joined together to destroy
    the planet Earth,
  No need to worry.
We'll all start again somewhere else in the grand universe.
  We'll have only lost a few million years.
There's plenty of time
  and no shortage of pain with which to fill it
    until you decide to be free.

STAR LOVE

There's a star in the sky tonight that's shining a special
    message to you.
  Yes, you.
  No one else.
You didn't know that you matter that much to a star?
  You didn't recognize your specialness in the heart of that
      star?
  You didn't know that the star loves you?
How did you miss it?
Did someone forget to teach you? Or did you fail to hear?
Pity the star. Its messages are rarely received,
  its love letters seldom opened.
How is it you say that you missed last night's love?

THE MYSTERY

Why am I here?
  Why not?
Is it an honor or an insult to be here?
  Both.
Why am I here?
  To learn.
And how do I learn?
  By remembering.
Remembering the forgotten?
  Of course. Only that which is already known is capable of
    freeing you.
And what is it that I know?
  Who it is that you are.
And who am I?
  Ah! That is why you're here. Remember . . . remember
    . . . remember . . .

THE CENTIPEDE

How many legs does it take a centipede to walk from here to
    there?
One hundred, you assume. And you are wrong.
  It takes two hundred. All that he has and a hundred more.
For you it takes only a hundred and two legs.
  All that you have and a hundred more.
Be thankful to your fifty friends.

THE CHRIST WITHIN

There is a Christ within you.
  Not a Jesus, for he was a man.
  A Christ who is of pure wisdom, pure wholeness,
  pure Godliness, pure consciousness.
What do you say when he calls to you each day?
You didn't hear him this morning?
  You forgot to check your mail?
  You let the phone ring unanswered?
No wonder you did not know he tried to reach you this
    morning.
No matter. He'll try again tomorrow.

BE CAREFUL WHAT YOU BELIEVE

Be careful what you believe.
Do you believe that
  Death is the end of life?
  Life is the beginning of death?
  What begins must end and what ends had a beginning?
Then you must also believe
  That God is this, and God is that,
    and God is surely not the man who robbed you
    or the woman who scorned you.
Be careful what you believe.
  One pure belief can set you free.
  One foul belief can lead you into a putrid forest of a
    thousand more.

111

FIREFLIES

Fireflies light up from within.
Try it.

THE MUSEUM

Works of priceless art hang on the walls of the gallery.
You imagine that they were created by a man a hundred years
    ago,
  and you fail to see that that very painting is being created
    now
  as you gaze upon it.
You are the creator, the creation, and the creating.
If only you understood that, peace and truth would reign
  and the world would be free from the weight of darkness.

ANGEL TALK

Notice the babble in the airport or the subway, and notice your
    reaction.
You do not struggle to understand Hindi or Arabic or
    Japanese.
  It seems pointless to try to comprehend.
  Shrug it off.
  It's babble.
  If your ears cannot comprehend it, it surely cannot be very
    important.
When angels talk, you shrug even harder.
When we tell you that you are made of Light,
  you say we speak of simple electricity
    and let it go at that.
When we tell you that you are God,
  you hear our words as idle poetry
    and call us the heavens' romantics.
When we send you miracles,
  you call our gifts coincidence
    so that you need not bow before them.
Angel talk—you act as though it is just more noise
  in an already very noisy,
    very dirty,
      very dangerous subway station.
Struggle to understand us and escape the sub-way.

THE TRIAL

The next time you stand before a judge
  notice that the judge is yourself.
It is always so . . .
  no exceptions.
Make peace with yourself
  and your sentence shall be light.
Love yourself
  and your reward shall be Light.

THE CORNER

Crouching in the dark corner of your room
  You wait.
  You wait for me to come.
You wait as though you were blind
  and only my touch can heal you.
You wait as though you were deaf
  and it's only my voice you can hear.
You wait as though you are crippled
  and only my legs will give you strength.
You wait . . .
  As though you were not me.

THE SONG OF THE SOUL

Sometimes you hear the music of your soul.
Listen in silence for her song.
Let it become your lullaby.
Let it rock you to sleep
  And gently arouse you from your dreams.
Your soul sings to you every moment of every day.
  She is a gentle mother
  whose voice is soft and clear.
Quiet now.
  Hush the abrasive thoughts of your mind.
  Hush the accusations you fling at yourself.
  Hush the bitterness and malice.
  Hush now.
Be loved.
Be healed by her song.

THE SERPENTS

All that you do not know
  Is known inside of you.
The wisdom you seek
  is held within you
  in a silver chalice
  near your heart.
The gate to the room of knowledge is guarded by serpents
  Whose venom will kill.
They guard your wisdom
  Against you.
It is your wisdom,
  yet you must be prevented from raping it.
  So your serpents frighten you away from their door.
Conquer your fear and their venom will become the nectar of
    the gods,
  and they will take your hand and usher you in
  to your wisdom.

THE PEACEFUL RESPITE

I provide a shelter from your inner cold.
  I provide a harbor in the midst of your self-inflicted
    hurricane.
  I provide a lifeline in the turbulent waters you inhabit.
I provide all these to you
  In response to your plea: "Help me. Help me."
When you know that which you must know,
  you will be a harbor to me.
At that time you will be my peaceful respite.
At that time you will be the home to which I lovingly return.

CRY

There is little time left for faint cries
  for crying alone
    for crying off key.
Cry loud
  and long
    and clear
Together with others who cry for their pain
  for their lost years
    for their souls.
Scream out your name.
  Scream out your pain.
There is little time left for plaintive moans and wistful wails.
Cry out. Let your cry be heard.
Let your cry become a bird
  one of the flock
    flying home.

TWO LOVERS

We cannot be two, you and I.
For there is no two
  No such being as two.
Either we are one, or we are split into many.
As we lie here together, me gazing into your eyes, you into
    mine,
  know that we are not two, you and I.
  We are either one or millions.
I embrace you as my love—the love within me,
  and you become everyone, all who have ever lived.
As I balk, "No, you are not everyone!", then I feel my soul
    wrenched
  into thousands of fragments.
    Not-this
      Not-that
        Not-this
          Not-that.
The list of who you are not never ends
  and you dim before my eyes.
Our love fades into another not
  and we are two.
Return to me. I embrace you as all.

THE LIGHT

The light which shines within your eyes
Is the result of a seed that God planted long ago.
The seed germinated
  and grew
    until it became a seedling of purity.
It was then planted in hard and rocky soil,
  in barren ground.
That it lives on is God's will and God's miracle.
Your hands can plow,
  your mind can weed,
    your heart can fertilize.
Or your hands can choke,
  your mind can deny
    and your heart can ignore.
You believe that you are unfit soil for the light of God.
Yet you are just that—soil for the light of God.

HAPPINESS

There is a happiness that comes when you have no attachment
That is profound and deep.
It cares not to be happy about something
   or to be delighted with something
      or to be excited over something.
This happiness can lift you into my realm,
   feed you at my table,
      fill you with my wine
         and satiate all heavenly hungers.
My happiness cannot war against your lust for earthly
      pleasures and material gains.
My happiness cannot substitute itself in the place of your
      follies.
My happiness cannot invade your illusions.
For one moment, drop your illusory needs.
   Release your wants and desires.
Imagine for just one moment that their fulfillment matters not.
Just let them lie,
   let them sleep
      for just a single moment.
And now look upward.
Can you see it? A glimpse of my happiness?
Come. Feast. It is yours.

A SONG OF YULETIDE PEACE

The yuletide season dawns.
In its early morning light it brings the hope of peace.
  Once again, in one more year,
  peace is offered to the world as a dream.
The world itself breathes peace.
  You breathe peace.
   You walk in peace.
Yet that very peace is like an alien in your land,
  a stranger in your home,
  an enemy in your camp.
It is still just a dream, this elusive peace.
Like love itself, peace cannot intrude.
Peace cannot demand entrance into your waking.
Peace cannot defeat your defeating it.
Peace can only come as a dream
  beckoning to you
   offering
    whispering.
It is not you who hopes for peace.
It is Peace who hopes that you will receive her.

Becca Zinn is a bright star in Uni★Sun's constellation of chan-
nelled writers. Her first book, *Stardust,* has inspired many read-
ers, and we expect Becca to start work on a third book soon.

In the meantime, we at Uni★Sun will do our best to publish
books and offer products that make a real contribution to the
global spiritual awakening that has already begun on this planet.
For a free copy of our catalogue, please write to:

Uni★Sun
P.O. Box 25421
Kansas City, Missouri
64119
U.S.A.